VODKA

VODKA

spruce

An Hachette UK Company
www.hachette.co.uk

First published in Great Britain in 2014 by
Spruce, a division of Octopus Publishing Group Ltd
Carmelite House, 50 Victoria Embankment, London EC4Y 0DZ
www.octopusbooks.co.uk
www.octopusbooksusa.com

This edition published in 2018.

Distributed in the US by Hachette Book Group
1290 Avenue of the Americas, 4th and 5th Floors, New York, NY 10104

Distributed in Canada by Canadian Manda Group
664 Annette Street, Toronto, Ontario, Canada M6S 2C8

These recipes have previously been published by Hamlyn.

ISBN 978-1-84601-574-8

A CIP catalogue record for this book is available from the British Library

Printed and bound in China

10 9 8 7 6 5 4 3 2 1

Notes for American readers: The measure that has been used in the recipes is based on a
bar jigger, which is 45 ml (1½ fl oz). If preferred, a different volume can be used providing the
proportions are kept constant within a drink and suitable adjustments are made to spoon
measurements, where they occur.
Standard level spoon measurements are used in all recipes: 1 tablespoon = one 15 ml spoon.
1 teaspoon = one 5 ml spoon. Imperial and metric measurements have been given in some of
the recipes. Use one set of measurements only and not a mixture of both.

UK	US
caster sugar	granulated sugar
cocktail cherries	maraschino cherries
cocktail stick	toothpick
double cream	heavy cream
drinking chocolate	presweetened cocoa powder
icing sugar	confectioners' sugar
jug	pitcher
lemon rind	lemon peel or zest
single cream	light cream
soda water	club soda

Contents

The Moscow Mule was arguably the first true vodka cocktail and since its invention in 1941, a complete repertoire of classics has developed from the sophisticated Vodka Gibson to the robust Bloody Mary and from the richly flavoured Black Russian to the refreshing Screwdriver. All these great favourites are included here.

This sparkling collection of lively cocktails will make any party a sure-fire success, from the tried-and-tested Vodka Martini to the up-to-the-minute Millennium Cocktail. In fact, just serving them will turn any occasion into a special celebration.

The versatility of vodka is amply demonstrated here. Mix it with fruit, fruit juice, liqueurs, cream, ice cream or spices to set the taste buds tingling. Whether you choose Frozen Steppes, Siamese Slammer or Caribbean Cruise, you will be transported with delight.

Introduction

Just as Scotland and Ireland both claim to have invented whisky, Russia and Poland argue over the origins of vodka. The Poles reckon that they were distilling vodka as early as the eighth century, but as the spirit they produced was distilled from wine, it was probably closer to brandy. By the eleventh century, they were producing a medicinal spirit called gorzalka, which would be more or less recognizable as vodka. The first documented production of vodka in Russia dates from the end of the ninth century, although the first known distillery, at Khylnovsk, was not recorded until 1174. The word vodka, meaning 'little water', is derived from the Russian *voda* – water – but as it is called *wodka* in Poland, this is an unreliable guide to its origins. In fact, the word vodka was not officially recognized until the end of the nineteenth century, when state distilleries and standard production techniques were introduced in Russia.

Whatever its origins, the vodka of the distant past was very different from the drink produced today. It was originally distilled from potato mash – traditionally, rotting potatoes – and because of impurities and sometimes a perfectly foul taste, it was often flavoured with herbs, spices, honey, fruit, nuts and a variety of aromatics. Production techniques, including pot distillation in the fifteenth century and charcoal filtering in the eighteenth, improved over the years and vodka also began to be produced from grains, such as wheat, or molasses.

The drink that had been dubbed by the British Ambassador in the fourteenth century as 'the Russian national drink,' was first exported in 1505, to Sweden. However, it was not until the years following the Bolshevik Revolution that vodka really took off in the West. When the Communists took over the distilleries, many private vodka-makers left Russia. One of them, Smirnoff, travelled to the United States via Paris and, in 1934, the first American vodka distillery was established. Even then, interest in the spirit was limited and it was not until the swinging sixties that vodka became a popular drink among the newly independent younger generation. This coincided, perhaps not by chance, with the rediscovery of cocktails, which had gone into something of a decline following World War II.

Western vodka undergoes strict processes of distillation and filtering, which not only take out impurities, but also the natural flavour. Flavourless, colourless and odourless, it is the perfect partner for other spirits and flavourings – with the additional advantage of leaving no tell-tale signs of having been drinking on the breath. Vodka cocktails are the younger cousins of the classics based on gin, whisky or brandy that had their heyday during the 1920s, but they have become firm favourites in bars and hotels across the world. Things have now gone full circle and it has become trendy to drink flavoured vodkas once again. Some of these modern flavourings, such as chilli, seem bizarre to contemplate and it is difficult to think of many palatable cocktails based on them. However, other more traditional flavours, such as orange or peach, could provide an interesting base for a range of popular cocktail recipes.

Sugar Syrup

This may be used instead of sugar to sweeten cocktails and to give them more body. It can be bought, but is simple to make at home.

Put 4 tablespoons of caster sugar and 4 tablespoons water in a small pan and stir over a low heat until the sugar has dissolved. Bring to the boil and boil, without stirring, for 1–2 minutes. Store in a sterilized bottle in the refrigerator for up to 2 months.

Classics

Astronaut

Bloody Mary

Le Mans

Hair Raiser

Screwdriver

Godmother

Harvey Wallbanger

Vodka Collins

Vodka Gibson

Vodka Sazerac

Xantippe

Inspiration

Iceberg

Haven

Vodka Salty Dog

White Spider

Vodka Grasshopper

Moscow Mule

White Russian

Black Russian

Long Island Iced Tea

Bullshot

Astronaut

8–10 cracked ice cubes
½ measure white rum
½ measure vodka
½ measure fresh lemon
    juice
1 dash passion fruit juice
lemon wedge, to
    decorate

Put 4–5 ice cubes into a cocktail shaker and add the rum, vodka, lemon juice and passion fruit juice. Fill an old-fashioned glass with the remaining ice cubes. Shake the cocktail until a frost forms, then strain it into the glass. Decorate with the lemon wedge and serve.

Serves 1

Bloody Mary

4–5 ice cubes
juice of ½ lemon
½ teaspoon horseradish
    sauce
2 drops Worcestershire
    sauce
1 drop Tabasco sauce
2 measures thick tomato
    juice
2 measures vodka
salt and cayenne pepper

to decorate (optional)
celery stick, with the
    leaves left on
lemon or lime slice

There are many variations on this classic cocktail, invented in 1921 at Harry's Bar in Paris. Spicy or mild, naked or decorated, and the best vodka you can get hold of – although experts cannot agree which this is.

Put the ice cubes into a cocktail shaker. Pour the lemon juice, horseradish sauce, Worcestershire sauce, Tabasco sauce, tomato juice and vodka over the ice. Shake until a frost forms. Pour into a tall glass, add a pinch of salt and a pinch of cayenne and decorate with a celery stick and a lemon or lime slice, if you like.

Serves 1

Le Mans

2–3 cracked ice cubes
1 measure Cointreau
½ measure vodka
soda water
lemon slice, to decorate

Put the cracked ice into a tall glass. Add the Cointreau and vodka, stir and top up with soda water. Float the lemon slice on the top.

Serves 1

Hair Raiser

1–2 cracked ice cubes
1 measure vodka
1 measure sweet
    vermouth
1 measure tonic water
lemon and lime rind
    spirals, to decorate

Put the cracked ice into a tall
glass and pour over the vodka,
vermouth and tonic. Stir lightly.
Decorate with the lemon and
lime rind spirals and serve
with a straw.

Serves 1

Tip
To make cracked ice, put
some ice cubes into a
strong polythene bag
and hit the bag with a
rolling pin.

Screwdriver

2–3 ice cubes
1½ measures vodka
freshly squeezed orange
juice

Put the ice cubes into a tumbler.
Add the vodka, top up with
orange juice and stir lightly.

Serves 1

Variation

Substitute apple juice for
the orange juice.
Decorate with a mint sprig.

Godmother

2–3 cracked ice cubes
1½ measures vodka
½ measure Amaretto di
Saronno

Put the ice cubes into a tumbler.
Add the vodka and Amaretto. Stir
lightly and serve.

Serves 1

Variation

To make a Godchild,
shake 1 measure each of
vodka, Amaretto and
double cream with ice.
Strain into a cocktail
glass and serve.

Harvey Wallbanger

6 ice cubes
1 measure vodka
3 measures fresh
    orange juice
1–2 teaspoons Galliano
orange slices, to
    decorate

This is a cocktail from the 1960s, named after a Californian surfer called Harvey who drank so many Screwdrivers topped with Galliano that, as he tried to find his way out of the bar, he banged and bounced from one wall to the other.

Put half the ice cubes into a cocktail shaker and the remainder into a tall glass. Add the vodka and orange juice to the cocktail shaker. Shake well for about 30 seconds, then strain into the glass. Float the Galliano on top. Decorate with orange slices and serve with straws.

Serves 1

Vodka Collins

6 ice cubes
2 measures vodka
juice of 1 lime
1 teaspoon caster sugar
soda water

to decorate
lemon or lime slice
maraschino cherry

Put half the ice cubes into a cocktail shaker and add the vodka, lime juice and sugar and shake until a frost forms. Strain into a large tumbler, add the remaining ice and top up with soda water. Decorate with lemon or lime slices and a cherry.

Serves 1

Vodka Gibson

6 ice cubes
1 measure vodka
½ measure dry vermouth
pearl onion

Put the ice cubes into a cocktail shaker and add the vodka and vermouth. Shake until a frost forms, then strain into a cocktail glass and decorate with the pearl onion.

Serves 1

Vodka Sazerac

1 sugar cube
2 drops Angostura bitters
3 drops Pernod
2–3 ice cubes
2 measures vodka
lemonade

Put the sugar cube into an old-fashioned glass and shake the bitters on to it. Add the Pernod and swirl it about so that it clings to the side of the glass. Drop in the ice cubes and pour in the vodka. Top up with lemonade, then stir gently.

Serves 1

Xantippe

4–5 ice cubes
1 measure cherry brandy
1 measure yellow
    Chartreuse
2 measures vodka

Put the ice cubes into a mixing glass. Pour the cherry brandy, Chartreuse and vodka over the ice and stir vigorously. Strain into a chilled cocktail glass.

Serves 1

Tip

Yellow Chartreuse is a herb-based liqueur made by French monks. It has a lower alcoholic content than the green variety.

Inspiration

4–5 ice cubes
½ measure Bénédictine
½ measure dry vermouth
2 measures vodka
lime rind spiral, to
    decorate

Put the ice cubes into a mixing glass. Pour the Bénédictine, vermouth and vodka over the ice. Stir vigorously, then strain into a chilled cocktail glass and decorate with the lime spiral.

Serves 1

Iceberg

4–6 ice cubes
1½ measures vodka
1 dash Pernod

Put the ice cubes into an old-fashioned glass. Pour in the vodka and add a dash of Pernod.

Serves 1

Haven

2–3 ice cubes
1 tablespoon grenadine
1 measure Pernod
1 measure vodka
soda water

Put the ice cubes into an old-fashioned glass. Dash the grenadine over the ice, then pour in the Pernod and vodka. Top up with soda water.

Serves 1

Vodka Salty Dog

salt
6–8 ice cubes
1 measure vodka
4 measures grapefruit
    juice

Salt the rim of a large goblet and
fill with ice. Add the vodka and
grapefruit juice and stir.

Serves 1

White Spider

2 measures vodka
1 measure clear crème
    de menthe
crushed ice (optional)

Pour the vodka and crème de
menthe into a cocktail shaker.
Shake and pour into a chilled
cocktail glass or over crushed ice.

Serves 1

Vodka
Grasshopper

1½ measures vodka
1½ measures green
    crème de menthe
1½ measures crème de
    cacao
crushed ice

Pour the vodka, crème de menthe
and crème de cacao into a
cocktail shaker half-filled with ice.
Shake and strain into a chilled
cocktail glass.

Serves 1

Moscow Mule

3–4 cracked ice cubes
2 measures vodka
juice of 2 limes
ginger beer
lime or orange slices,
    to decorate

This cocktail is one of those happy accidents. It was invented in 1941 by an employee of a US drinks firm in conjunction with a Los Angeles bar owner who was overstocked with ginger beer.

Put the cracked ice into a cocktail shaker. Add the vodka and lime juice and shake until a frost forms. Pour into a tall glass, top up with ginger beer and stir gently. Decorate with lime or orange slices.

Serves 1

White Russian

classics

6 cracked ice cubes
1 measure vodka
1 measure Tía María
1 measure milk or double
      cream

Put half the ice cubes into a cocktail shaker and add the vodka, Tía María and milk or double cream. Shake until a frost forms. Put the remaining ice cubes into a tall narrow glass and strain the cocktail over them. Serve with a straw.

Serves 1

Black Russian

4–6 cracked ice cubes
2 measures vodka
1 measure Kahlúa coffee
      liqueur
chocolate stick, to
      decorate (optional)

Put the cracked ice into a short glass. Add the vodka and Kahlúa and stir. Decorate with a chocolate stick, if you like.

Serves 1

Long Island Iced Tea

6 cracked ice cubes
½ measure vodka
½ measure gin
½ measure white rum
½ measure tequila
½ measure Cointreau
1 measure lemon juice
½ teaspoon sugar syrup
   (see page 7)
cola, to top up
lemon wedge, to
   decorate

Put half the ice cubes into a mixing glass. Add the vodka, gin, rum, tequila, Cointreau, lemon juice and sugar syrup. Stir well, then strain into a tall glass almost filled with ice. Top up with cola and decorate with the wedge of lemon. Serve with a straw.

Serves 1

Bullshot

6 ice cubes (optional)
1½ measures vodka
4 measures beef
    consommé (hot or
    chilled)
dash of Worcestershire
    sauce
salt and pepper

Put the ice cubes, if using, into a cocktail shaker and add the vodka, consommé and Worcestershire sauce and season lightly with salt and pepper. Shake well. Strain into a large glass or a handled glass, if serving hot.

Serves 1

Variation

This is said to be a good hangover cure. As a variation, try 1 measure vodka, 1 measure tomato juice and 1 measure beef consommé. Mix the ingredients in a tall glass half-filled with ice. Add a squeeze of lemon.

Party Cocktails

Vodka Martini

Vodka Sour

Blue Champagne

Head-over-Heels

Millennium Cocktail

Bellini-tini

Road Runner

One of Those

Sea Breeze

Cosmopolitan

Madras

Machete

Vodka Twister Fizz

Down-under Fizz

Vodka Limeade

Vodka, Lime & Soda

Snapdragon

Polish Honey Drink

Warsaw Cocktail

Vodka Martini

4–5 cracked ice cubes
¼ measure dry vermouth
3 measures vodka
green olive or a twist of
    lemon rind, to decorate

**In some circles this
concoction is known as
a Kangaroo.**

Put the ice cubes into a mixing
glass. Pour the vermouth and
vodka over the ice and stir
vigorously. Strain into a chilled
cocktail glass, drop in the olive
or decorate with a twist of
lemon rind.

Serves 1

Vodka Sour

4–5 ice cubes
2 measures vodka
½ measure sugar syrup
   (see page 7)
1 egg white
1½ measures fresh
   lemon juice
3 drops Angostura
   bitters, to decorate

Put the ice cubes into a cocktail shaker, add the vodka, sugar syrup, egg white and lemon juice and shake until a frost forms. Pour without straining into a cocktail glass and shake 3 drops of Angostura bitters on the top to decorate.

Serves 1

Blue Champagne

4–6 ice cubes
1 measure vodka
2 tablespoons fresh
   lemon juice
2–3 dashes triple sec
2–3 dashes blue curaçao
chilled Champagne, to
   top up

Put the ice cubes into a cocktail shaker, add the vodka, lemon juice, triple sec and blue curaçao and shake well. Strain into a Champagne flute and top up with Champagne.

Serves 1

Variation

Another vodka and Champagne combination is the Bucked-up Fizz. Pour 2 measures of orange juice and ½ measure of vodka into a Champagne flute. Top up with Champagne.

Head-over-Heels

4–5 ice cubes
juice of 1 lime or lemon
1 teaspoon sugar syrup
    (see page 7)
3 measures vodka
3 drops Angostura bitters
Champagne, to top up
strawberry, to decorate

Put the ice cubes into a cocktail shaker. Pour the lime or lemon juice, sugar syrup, vodka and bitters over the ice and shake until a frost forms. Pour without straining into a highball glass, top up with Champagne and decorate with a strawberry.

Serves 1

Millennium Cocktail

4–5 cracked ice cubes
1 measure vodka
1 measure fresh
  raspberry juice
1 measure fresh orange
  juice
4 measures Champagne
  or sparkling dry white
  wine, chilled

Put the ice cubes into a cocktail shaker, add the vodka, raspberry juice and orange juice and shake until a frost forms. Strain into a Champagne glass and pour in the Champagne.

Serves 1

Bellini-tini

4–5 cracked ice cubes
2 measures vodka
½ measure peach
    schnapps
1 teaspoon peach juice
Champagne, to top up
peach slices, to decorate

Put the ice cubes into a cocktail shaker and add the vodka, peach schnapps and peach juice. Shake until a frost forms. Strain into a chilled cocktail glass and top up with Champagne. Decorate with peach slices.

Serves 1

Road Runner

6 cracked ice cubes
2 measures vodka
1 measure Amaretto di
    Saronno
1 measure coconut milk
grated nutmeg, to
    decorate

Put the cracked ice into a
cocktail shaker and add the
vodka, Amaretto and coconut
milk. Shake until a frost forms,
then strain into a cocktail glass.
Sprinkle with a pinch of
grated nutmeg.

Serves 1

One of Those

4–6 ice cubes
1 measure vodka
4 measures cranberry
    juice
2 dashes Amaretto di
    Saronno
juice of ½ lime
lime slice, to decorate

Half-fill a highball glass with ice
cubes. Pour the vodka, cranberry
juice, Amaretto and lime juice
into a cocktail shaker. Shake
thoroughly, pour into the
highball glass and decorate with
a lime slice.

Serves 1

Variation

This tasty cocktail was
created in London by one
inventive Australian and
two thirsty Americans.

Sea Breeze

5 crushed ice cubes
1 measure vodka
1½ measures cranberry
   juice
1½ measures fresh
   grapefruit juice
lime slice, to decorate

**This is one of those drinks
that has changed
considerably over the
years. In the 1930s it was
made with gin rather than
vodka and with grenadine
and lemon juice instead of
cranberry juice and
grapefruit juice.**

Put the crushed ice into a tall
glass, pour over the vodka,
cranberry juice and grapefruit
juice and stir well. Decorate with
a lime slice and serve with
a straw.

Serves 1

Variation

To make a Cape
Cod(der), mix 1 measure
of vodka, 2 measures of
cranberry juice and add a
dash of lemon juice.

Cosmopolitan

6 cracked ice cubes
1 measure vodka
½ measure Cointreau
1 measure cranberry
   juice
juice of ½ lime
lime slice, to decorate

Put the cracked ice into a cocktail shaker and add the vodka, Cointreau, cranberry juice and lime juice. Shake until a frost forms. Strain into a cocktail glass and decorate with a lime slice.

Serves 1

Madras

6–8 ice cubes
1 measure vodka
1 measure orange juice
2 measures cranberry
    juice
orange or lime slice, to
    decorate

Half-fill a tall glass with ice. Pour
over the vodka, orange juice and
cranberry juice and decorate with
a fruit slice.

Serves 1

Machete

4–6 ice cubes
1 measure vodka
2 measures pineapple
   juice
3 measures tonic water

Fill a tall glass or wine glass with ice cubes. Pour the vodka, pineapple juice and tonic into a mixing glass. Stir, then pour into the glass.

Serves 1

Vodka Twister Fizz

4–5 ice cubes
juice of 1 lemon
½ teaspoon sugar syrup
(see page 7)
1 egg white
3 drops Pernod
3 measures vodka
ginger ale
lime slice, to decorate

Put the ice cubes into a cocktail shaker. Pour the lemon juice, sugar syrup, egg white, Pernod and vodka over the ice and shake until a frost forms. Pour without straining into a highball glass and top up with ginger ale. Stir once or twice and decorate with a lime slice.

Serves 1

Down-under Fizz

4–5 ice cubes
juice of 1 lemon
juice of ½ orange
½ teaspoon grenadine
3 measures vodka
soda water

Put the ice cubes into a cocktail shaker. Pour the lemon juice, orange juice, grenadine and vodka over the ice and shake until a frost forms. Pour without straining into a highball glass and top up with soda water. Serve with a straw.

Serves 1

Vodka Limeade

6 limes
125 g (4 oz) caster sugar
750 ml (1¼ pints) boiling
    water
salt
8 measures vodka
ice cubes
lime wedges, to decorate

Halve the limes, then squeeze the juice into a large jug. Put the squeezed halves into a heatproof bowl with the sugar and boiling water and leave to infuse for 15 minutes. Add a pinch of salt, give the infusion a good stir then strain it into the jug with the lime juice and add the vodka. Add 6 ice cubes, cover and refrigerate for 2 hours, or until chilled. To serve, place 3–4 ice cubes in each glass and pour the limeade over them. Decorate each glass with a lime wedge.

Serves 8

Tip

If you roll the whole limes around quite hard on a board with your hand, you will find that you get more juice from them.

Vodka, Lime & Soda

6–8 ice cubes
1 measure vodka
2 measures lime cordial
   or lime juice
soda water
lime slice, to decorate

Half-fill a tall glass with ice cubes. Pour in the vodka and lime cordial or lime juice, top up with soda water and stir. Decorate with a lime slice.

Serves 1

Variation

A quick fix of this combination is called a Cosmos. Pour 1 measure vodka and ½ measure freshly squeezed lime juice into a cocktail shaker half-filled with ice. Shake well and strain into a shot glass.

Snapdragon

4–6 ice cubes
2 measures vodka
4 measures green crème
    de menthe
soda water
mint sprigs, to decorate

Fill a highball glass with ice cubes. Add the vodka and crème de menthe and stir. Top up with soda water. Decorate with a mint sprig.

Serves 1

Polish Honey Drink

6 tablespoons clear honey
300 ml (½ pint) water
4 cloves
7.5 cm (3 inch) piece of cinnamon stick
1 vanilla pod
2 long lemon rind strips
2 long orange rind strips
1 bottle vodka (750 ml/1¼ pints)

Put the honey and water into a saucepan and heat gently until the honey has dissolved. Add the cloves, cinnamon stick, vanilla pod, lemon rind and orange rind. Bring to the boil and simmer for 5 minutes. Cover the pan, remove from the heat and leave to infuse for 1 hour. Strain and return to the rinsed pan. Add the vodka and bring to just below simmering point over a low heat and warm through for 5 minutes. Serve in warmed handled glasses or mugs.

Serves 8

Warsaw Cocktail

6 ice cubes
1 measure vodka
½ measure blackberry-
    flavoured brandy
½ measure dry vermouth
1 teaspoon fresh lemon
    juice

Put the ice cubes into a cocktail shaker and add the vodka, brandy, vermouth and lemon juice. Shake until a frost forms. Strain into a cocktail glass and serve.

Serves 1

Exotic & Fruity

Siamese Slammer

Cool Wind

Chi Chi

Blue Moon

Sloe Comfortable Screw

Cranberry Crush

Vodka & Watermelon Crush

Frozen Steppes

Creamsickle

Vodka Daiquiri

Cherry Vodka Julep

Melon Ball

Caribbean Cruise

Monkey's Delight

Sex on the Beach

Hairy Fuzzy Navel

Vodka Caipirinha

Mudslide

Russian Coffee

Hawaiian Vodka

Lemon Drop

Kamikaze

Siamese Slammer

3 measures vodka
juice of 2 oranges
1 small ripe papaya,
    peeled and chopped
1 banana, sliced
juice of 1 lime
3 measures sugar syrup
    (see page 7)
8 crushed ice cubes
4 papaya slices, to
    decorate

Put all the ingredients into
a blender and process until
smooth. Serve in tall glasses,
each decorated with a slice
of papaya.

Serves 4

Cool Wind

4–5 ice cubes
1 measure dry vermouth
juice of ½ grapefruit
½ teaspoon Cointreau
3 measures vodka

Put the ice cubes into a mixing glass. Pour the vermouth, grapefruit juice, Cointreau and vodka over the ice. Stir gently, then strain into a chilled cocktail glass.

Serves 1

Chi Chi

2 measures vodka
1 measure coconut
  cream
4 measures pineapple
  juice
6 crushed ice cubes

to decorate
pineapple slice
maraschino cherry

Put the vodka, coconut cream, pineapple juice and crushed ice into a blender and process until smooth. Pour into a tall glass and decorate with a slice of pineapple and a cherry.

Serves 1

exotic & fruity

Blue Moon

5 cracked ice cubes
¾ measure vodka
¾ measure tequila
1 measure blue curaçao
lemonade

Put half the ice into a mixing glass and add the vodka, tequila and blue curaçao. Stir to mix. Put the remaining ice into a tall glass and strain in the cocktail. Top up with lemonade and serve with a straw.

Serves 1

Sloe Comfortable Screw

6–8 ice cubes
½ measure sloe gin
½ measure Southern
   Comfort
1 measure vodka
2½ measures orange
   juice

The name of this drink is an easy way of remembering what goes into it. Sloe for the sloe gin, Comfortable for the Southern Comfort and Screw, short for Screwdriver – vodka and orange juice.

Variation

To make a Sloe Comfortable Screw Up Against the Wall, mix the drink as above and top with Galliano. The final part of the name derives from the place where the tall, slender bottle of Galliano is usually kept in a bar.

Half-fill a tall glass with ice cubes. Pour the sloe gin, Southern Comfort, vodka and orange juice into the glass and stir well.

Serves 1

73

Cranberry Crush

600 ml (1 pint) cranberry
   juice
600 ml (1 pint) fresh
   orange juice
150 ml (¼ pint) water
½ teaspoon ground
   ginger
½ teaspoon mixed spice
sugar
1 bottle vodka
   (750 ml/1¼ pints)

to decorate
kumquats
cranberries
mint sprigs

Place the cranberry juice, orange juice, water, ginger and mixed spice in a saucepan and bring to the boil over a low heat. Stir in sugar to taste, then simmer for 5 minutes. Remove from the heat and stir in the vodka. Pour into punch cups, decorate with kumquats, cranberries and mint sprigs. Alternatively, serve chilled for a summer party.

Serves 10

Vodka & Watermelon Crush

1 large or 2 small ripe
    watermelons, chilled
300 ml (½ pint) fresh
    orange juice
juice of 1 lime
3 measures vodka
sugar
crushed ice
watermelon slices,
    to decorate

Cut the watermelon into quarters and remove the skin and seeds. Roughly chop the flesh and put it into a blender or food processor with the orange juice, lime juice and vodka. Add sugar to taste and process until smooth. Fill 2–3 glasses with crushed ice and pour in the drink. Add a watermelon slice to each glass to decorate.

Serves 2–3

Frozen Steppes

1 measure vodka
1 measure dark crème
    de cacao
1 scoop vanilla ice cream
maraschino cherry, to
    decorate

Put the vodka, crème de cacao and ice cream into a blender and process for a few seconds. Pour into a large wine glass and decorate with a cherry.

Serves 1

Creamsickle

6 cracked ice cubes
1 measure vodka
1 measure triple sec
1 measure white crème
    de cacao
1 measure single cream

Put the cracked ice into a cocktail shaker and add the vodka, triple sec, crème de cacao and cream. Shake until a frost forms, then pour into a highball glass.

Serves 1

Vodka Daiquiri

exotic & fruity

6 cracked ice cubes
1 measure vodka
1 teaspoon sugar
juice of ½ lime or lemon

Put the cracked ice into a cocktail shaker and add the vodka, sugar and lime or lemon juice. Shake until a frost forms. Strain into a cocktail glass.

Serves 1

Variation

To make a frozen daiquiri, combine the vodka, sugar and lime or lemon juice in a blender with a handful of crushed ice. Process for a few seconds on low speed, then at high speed until firm. Decorate with a slice of lime and a cherry and serve with a straw.

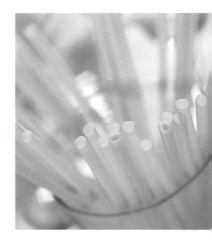

Cherry Vodka Julep

8 cracked ice cubes
juice of ½ lemon
1 teaspoon sugar or
    sugar syrup (see
    page 7)
1 teaspoon grenadine
1 measure cherry brandy
3 measures vodka
1 measure sloe gin

to decorate
1 lemon slice
1 orange slice

Fill a tall glass with cracked ice. Put 3–4 ice cubes into a mixing glass and pour in the lemon juice, sugar or sugar syrup, grenadine, cherry brandy, vodka and sloe gin. Stir, then strain into the ice-filled glass. Decorate with the lemon and orange slices.

Serves 1

Melon Ball

5 cracked ice cubes
1 measure vodka
1 measure Midori
1 measure orange juice,
    plus extra for
    topping up

to decorate
orange slice
small ball of banana

Put the cracked ice into a tall glass or goblet. Pour the vodka, Midori and orange juice into a cocktail shaker. Shake well to mix, then strain into the glass. Top up with more orange juice if necessary. Decorate with the fruit and serve with a straw.

Serves 1

Caribbean Cruise

10–12 ice cubes
1 measure vodka
¼ measure light rum
¼ measure coconut rum
1 dash of grenadine
2 measures pineapple
    juice
pineapple slice, to
    decorate

Put 6 ice cubes into a cocktail shaker and add the vodka, both kinds of rum and a dash of grenadine. Shake until a frost forms. Half-fill a tall glass with ice cubes, strain the cocktail over the ice and add the pineapple juice. Decorate with a pineapple slice.

Serves 1

Monkey's Delight

1 measure vodka
½ measure crème de banane
½ measure dark crème de cacao
1 banana
2 scoops vanilla ice cream
½ measure single cream

Put the vodka, crème de banane, crème de cacao, ¾ of the banana, the ice cream and cream in a blender and process until smooth. Pour into a tall glass. Decorate with the reserved banana, cut into slices.

Serves 1

Sex on the Beach

3 ice cubes
½ measure vodka
½ measure peach
   schnapps
1 measure cranberry
   juice
1 measure orange juice
1 measure pineapple
   juice (optional)
maraschino cherry, to
   decorate

Put the ice into a cocktail shaker and add the vodka, peach schnapps, cranberry juice, orange juice and pineapple juice, if using. Shake until a frost forms. Pour into a tall glass, decorate with the cherry and serve with a straw.

Serves 1

Hairy Fuzzy Navel

6 cracked ice cubes
1 measure peach
    schnapps
1½ measures vodka
1 tablespoon orange
    juice

Put the cracked ice into a cocktail shaker and add the peach schnapps, vodka and orange juice. Shake until a frost forms, then strain into a cocktail glass.

Serves 1

Variation

A Fuzzy Navel is made without the vodka.

Vodka Caipirinha

6 lime wedges
2 teaspoons brown sugar
2 measures vodka
crushed ice

This is a vodka variation of the authentic cocktail which is traditionally made with cachaça, a Brazilian spirit made from rum and sugar cane.

Place 3 of the lime wedges in a large tumbler or old-fashioned glass and add the brown sugar and vodka. Mix well, mashing the lime wedges slightly to release a little juice. Top up with crushed ice and decorate with the remaining lime wedges.

Serves 1

Mudslide

10 cracked ice cubes
1 measure vodka
1 measure Kahlúa
1 measure Baileys Irish
    Cream

Put 6 cracked ice cubes into a cocktail shaker and add the vodka, Kahlúa and Baileys. Shake until a frost forms. Strain into a tumbler and add the remaining cracked ice.

Serves 1

Russian Coffee

½ measure vodka
½ measure coffee liqueur
½ measure double cream
crushed ice

Put the vodka, coffee liqueur, cream and crushed ice into a blender and process for about 15 seconds. Strain into a cocktail glass and serve.

Serves 1

Tip

Before taking a sip of this drink, why not toast to your health with the customary Russian and Polish toast *na zdrowie*?

Hawaiian Vodka

4–5 ice cubes
1 measure pineapple
   juice
juice of 1 lemon
juice of 1 orange
1 teaspoon grenadine
3 measures vodka
lemon slice, to decorate

Put the ice cubes into a cocktail shaker. Add the pineapple juice, lemon juice, orange juice, grenadine and vodka and shake until a frost forms. Strain into a tumbler, decorate with a lemon slice and serve with a straw.

Serves 1

Lemon Drop

6 cracked ice cubes
1 measure vodka
lemon wedge
sugar, for dipping

Put the cracked ice into a cocktail shaker and add the vodka. Strain into a shot glass. Dip the lemon wedge in the sugar. Drink the vodka, then suck on the lemon immediately.

Serves 1

Kamikaze

6 cracked ice cubes
½ measure vodka
½ measure triple sec
½ measure lime juice

Put the cracked ice into a cocktail shaker and add the vodka, triple sec and lime juice. Shake until a frost forms, then strain into a shot glass.

Serves 1

INDEX

Acknowledgements

Octopus Publishing Group
Ltd./Jean Cazals 45
/Sandra Lane 95
/Neil Mersh 19, 23, 41, 46, 49,
58, 59, 83, 89, 93
/Peter Myers 38, 55, 71
/William Reavell Cover, 2, 3, 5,
6-7, 8, 11, 13, 16, 21, 25,
27, 29, 30, 33, 34, 43, 51,
53, 57, 61, 64, 66, 68, 72,
75, 77, 80, 84

RUM

RUM

spruce

An Hachette UK Company
www.hachette.co.uk

First published in Great Britain in 2014 by
Spruce, a division of Octopus Publishing Group Ltd
Carmelite House, 50 Victoria Embankment, London EC4Y 0DZ
www.octopusbooks.co.uk
www.octopusbooksusa.com

This edition published in 2018.

Copyright © Octopus Publishing Group Ltd 2014, 2018

Distributed in the US by Hachette Book Group
1290 Avenue of the Americas, 4th and 5th Floors, New York, NY 10104

Distributed in Canada by Canadian Manda Group
664 Annette Street, Toronto, Ontario, Canada M6S 2C8

These recipes have previously been published by Hamlyn.

ISBN 978-1-84601-574-8

A CIP catalogue record for this book is available from the British Library

Printed and bound in China

10 9 8 7 6 5 4 3 2 1

Notes for American readers: The measure that has been used in the recipes is based on a
bar jigger, which is 45 ml (1½ fl oz). If preferred, a different volume can be used providing the
proportions are kept constant within a drink and suitable adjustments are made to spoon
measurements, where they occur.
Standard level spoon measurements are used in all recipes: 1 tablespoon = one 15 ml spoon.
1 teaspoon = one 5 ml spoon. Imperial and metric measurements have been given in some of
the recipes. Use one set of measurements only and not a mixture of both.

UK	US
caster sugar	granulated sugar
cocktail cherries	maraschino cherries
cocktail stick	toothpick
double cream	heavy cream
drinking chocolate	presweetened cocoa powder
icing sugar	confectioners' sugar
jug	pitcher
lemon rind	lemon peel or zest
single cream	light cream
soda water	club soda

Contents

Introduction

Rum has a strange mixture of associations – from smugglers risking shipwreck off the Cornish coast and captured by the merciless militia men, or as the free tipple that kept the British Navy happy, to wealthy planters relaxing on sunny verandas leisurely sipping long fruit-bedecked concoctions.

Christopher Columbus is said to have introduced sugar cane to the Caribbean. While this may be mere legend, it is undoubtedly true that the Caribbean introduced the rest of the world to the spirit distilled from it – rum. By the 17th century distillation from sugar cane or its products was taking place in Hispaniola to produce a spirit that a contemporary described as 'hot, hellish and terrible'.

Over the years, it became more palatable, as new techniques were discovered –

cultured yeasts, the benefit of maturing in casks, improved filtration and, in the 1830s, the patent still. From being a rough spirit that colonists only drank for want of anything better, it became a popular drink, first in western Europe and later throughout the world. The right of sailors to a rum ration was enshrined by Britain's Royal Navy and was not abolished until the 20th century.

Rum is distilled from molasses and, in some cases, directly from the fermented juices of the sugar cane. To begin with, it is a colourless, high-strength spirit with little natural flavour. Caramel may then be added to give colour and some premium rums also acquire colour while maturing in oak casks. There are basically three types of rum – white, golden or light and dark. Various flavourings are also added and it is common for rums from different places to be blended.

Rum is produced wherever sugar cane grows, but arguably, the Caribbean produces the best and each island group has its own type. Martinique and Jamaica are well-known for pungent, sweet, heavy-bodied dark rums. Paler, drier and lighter golden rums are widely produced, especially in Cuba, Puerto Rico and Barbados. Puerto Rico is also the largest producer of white rum, but it is made in many other places, too.

White rum is a popular base for cocktails, as it blends easily with a wide range of flavours. Many classics – Daiquiri, Piña Colada, Blue Hawaiian and Mai Tai – are white rum cocktails. Darker rums combine superbly with fruit juices, especially lime, and are perfect for cold or hot punches. Some cocktails, such as the Zombie, are based on a mixture of different types of rum and, perhaps surprisingly, although it has a strong flavour itself, rum combines well with other spirits and liqueurs.

Sugar Syrup

This may be used instead of sugar to sweeten cocktails and to give them more body. It can be bought, but is simple to make at home.

Put 4 tablespoons of sugar and 4 tablespoons water in a small pan and stir over a low heat until the sugar has dissolved. Bring to the boil and boil, without stirring, for 1–2 minutes. Store in a sterilized bottle in the refrigerator for up to 2 months.

7

Daiquiris
& Zombies

Daiquiri

cracked ice
juice of 2 limes
1 teaspoon sugar syrup
(see page 7)
3 measures white rum

The Daiquiri was created by an American mining engineer working in Cuba in 1896. He was expecting VIP guests and his supplies of gin had run out, so he extemporized with rum – and created this classic cocktail.

Put lots of cracked ice into a cocktail shaker. Pour the lime juice, sugar syrup and rum over the ice. Shake thoroughly until a frost forms, then strain into a chilled cocktail glass.

Serves 1

Banana Daiquiri

3 ice cubes, cracked
2 measures white rum
½ measure banana
   liqueur
½ small banana
½ measure lime cordial

to decorate
1 teaspoon powdered
   sugar (optional)
slice of banana

Put the cracked ice in a margarita glass or tall goblet. Put the rum, banana liqueur, banana and lime cordial into a blender and blend for 30 seconds. Pour into the glass and decorate with the powdered sugar, if using, and banana slice.

Serves 1

Apricot Daiquiri

crushed ice
1 measure white rum
1 measure lemon juice
½ measure apricot liqueur
    or brandy
3 ripe apricots, peeled
    and pitted

to decorate
slice of apricot
cocktail cherry
mint sprig

This pretty pale-coloured cocktail looks particularly attractive if it is decorated by cutting the apricot slice in half and spearing the two halves and the cocktail cherry with a cocktail stick. Balance the cocktail stick across the glass on the rim.

Put some crushed ice into a blender. Add the rum, lemon juice, apricot liqueur or brandy and the apricots and blend for 1 minute, or until the mixture is smooth. Pour into a chilled cocktail glass and decorate with an apricot slice, a cocktail cherry and mint sprig.

Serves 1

14

Coconut Daiquiri

crushed ice
2 measures coconut
  liqueur
2 measures fresh
  lime juice
1 measure white rum
1 dash egg white
slice of lime, to decorate

Put the ice in a cocktail shaker and add all the ingredients. Shake vigorously until a frost forms. Strain and pour into a chilled cocktail glass. Decorate with a slice of lime.

Serves 1

Strawberry Daiquiri

1 measure white rum
½ measure crème
de fraises
½ measure fresh
lemon juice
4 ripe strawberries,
hulled
crushed ice

to decorate
slice of strawberry
mint sprig

This fruity cocktail is especially delicious if you make it with crème de fraises des bois, a wild strawberry liqueur.

Put the rum, crème de fraises, lemon juice, strawberries and ice into a food processor or blender and process at a slow speed for 5 seconds, then at high speed for about 20 seconds. Pour into a chilled glass and decorate with a strawberry slice and a mint sprig.

Serves 1

Frozen Pineapple Daiquiri

crushed ice
2–3 pineapple slices
½ measure fresh
    lime juice
1 measure white rum
¼ measure Cointreau
1 teaspoon sugar syrup
    (see page 7)
piece of pineapple,
    to decorate

Put some crushed ice into a blender and add the pineapple slices, lime juice, white rum, Cointreau and sugar syrup. Blend at the highest speed until smooth, then pour into a chilled cocktail glass. Decorate with a piece of fresh pineapple and serve with straw.

Serves 1

Melon Daiquiri

2 measures white rum
1 measure fresh
 lime juice
2 dashes Midori liqueur
2 scoops crushed ice

Put the white rum, lime juice and liqueur in a blender with the crushed ice and blend until smooth. Serve in a chilled goblet with straws.

Serves 1

Havana Zombie

4–5 ice cubes
juice of 1 lime
5 tablespoons
    pineapple juice
1 teaspoon sugar syrup
    (see page 7)
1 measure white rum
1 measure golden rum
1 measure dark rum

Put the ice cubes into a mixing glass. Pour the lime juice, pineapple juice, sugar syrup and rums over the ice and stir vigorously. Pour, without straining, into a tall glass.

Serves 1

Zombie

3 ice cubes, cracked
1 measure dark rum
1 measure white rum
½ measure golden rum
½ measure apricot brandy
juice of ½ lime
2 measures
    unsweetened
    pineapple juice
2 teaspoons powdered
    sugar

to decorate
slice of kiwi fruit
cocktail cherry
pineapple wedge
powdered sugar
    (optional)

Zombies contain all three types of rum – dark, golden and white. The darker rums are aged in charred oak casks while white rums are aged in stainless steel tanks.

Place a tall glass in the freezer so the outside becomes frosted. Put the ice into a cocktail shaker. Add the rums, apricot brandy, lime juice, pineapple juice and sugar. Shake to mix. Pour into the glass without straining. To decorate, spear the slice of kiwi fruit, cherry and pineapple with a cocktail stick and place it across the top of the glass, balanced on the rim. Sprinkle the powdered sugar over the top and serve.

Serves 1

Zombie Christophe

4–5 ice cubes
juice of 1 lime or lemon
juice of ½ orange
250 ml (8 fl oz)
     unsweetened
     pineapple juice
1 measure blue Curaçao
1 measure white rum
1 measure golden rum
½ measure dark rum

to decorate
slice of lime or lemon
mint sprig

Put the ice cubes into a mixing glass. Pour the lime or lemon juice, orange juice, pineapple juice, Curaçao, white and golden rums over the ice. Stir vigorously, then pour, without straining, into a tumbler. Top with the dark rum, stir gently and serve decorated with a slice of lime or lemon and a mint sprig.

Serves 1

Zombie Prince

crushed ice
juice of 1 lemon
juice of 1 orange
juice of ½ grapefruit
3 drops Angostura bitters
1 teaspoon soft
    brown sugar
1 measure white rum
1 measure golden rum
1 measure dark rum

to decorate
slices of lime
slices of orange

Put the crushed ice into a mixing glass. Pour the lemon, orange and grapefruit juices over the ice and splash in the bitters. Add the sugar and pour in the three rums. Stir vigorously, then pour, without straining, into a Collins glass. Decorate with slices of lime and orange.

Tip
A Collins glass is perfect for long drinks – the taller the better. They are always narrow with slightly tapered or perfectly straight sides.

Exotic Cocktails

Astronaut

Acapulco

Piña Colada

Coco Loco

Blue Hawaiian

Grenada

Mai Tai

Summertime

Banana Royal

Port Antonio

St Lucia

Bahamas

Serenade

Discovery Bay

Pussyfoot

Virgin's Prayer

Bombay Smash

Tropical Dream

Astronaut

8–10 ice cubes
½ measure white rum
½ measure vodka
½ measure lemon juice
1 dash passion fruit juice
lemon wedge, to
    decorate

Put 4–5 ice cubes into a cocktail shaker and add the rum, vodka, lemon and passion fruit juices. Fill an old-fashioned glass with 4–5 fresh ice cubes. Shake the cocktail until a frost forms, then strain it into the glass. Decorate with the lemon wedge.

Serves 1

Acapulco

crushed ice
1 measure tequila
1 measure white rum
2 measures
    pineapple juice
1 measure
    grapefruit juice
1 measure coconut milk
pineapple wedge,
    to decorate

Whenever a cocktail includes fruit juice, it always tastes better if the juice is freshly squeezed. Juice from a bottle or carton is better than nothing and the cocktail will still taste good.

Put some crushed ice into a cocktail shaker and pour in the tequila, rum, pineapple juice, grapefruit juice and coconut milk. Shake until a frost forms, then pour into a hurricane glass and decorate with a pineapple wedge. Serve with straws.

Serves 1

Piña Colada

cracked ice
1 measure white rum
2 measures coconut milk
(see opposite)
2 measures
pineapple juice

to decorate
slice of strawberry
slice of mango
slice of pineapple

Put some cracked ice, the rum, coconut milk and pineapple juice into a cocktail shaker. Shake lightly to mix. Strain into a large glass and decorate with the slices of strawberry, mango and pineapple.

Serves 1

Coco Loco

crushed ice
4 measures
   coconut water
1 measure coconut milk
1 measure apricot brandy
1 measure white rum
ground cinnamon

Coconut water is the thin liquid found inside a fresh coconut, whereas coconut milk is made by blending fresh coconut, grated coconut cream or desiccated coconut with hot water. Both coconut water and coconut milk are sold in cans.

Put some crushed ice into a blender and add the coconut water, coconut milk, apricot brandy and rum and blend at high speed. To serve, pour into a coconut shell and sprinkle with ground cinnamon.

Serves 1

Blue Hawaiian

crushed ice
1 measure white rum
½ measure blue Curaçao
2 measures
    pineapple juice
1 measure
    coconut cream
pineapple wedge,
    to decorate

The beautiful colour of this cocktail comes from the blue Curaçao, but the liqueur is actually made from bitter oranges.

Put some crushed ice into a blender and pour in the rum, blue Curaçao, pineapple juice and coconut cream. Blend at high speed for 20–30 seconds. Pour into a chilled cocktail glass and decorate with a pineapple wedge.

Serves 1

Grenada

4–5 ice cubes
juice of ½ orange
1 measure
    sweet vermouth
3 measures golden or
    dark rum
ground cinnamon

Put the ice cubes into a mixing glass. Pour the orange juice, vermouth and rum over the ice. Stir vigorously, then strain into a chilled cocktail glass. Sprinkle a little ground cinnamon on top.

Serves 1

Mai Tai

lightly beaten egg white
caster sugar, for frosting
1 measure white rum
½ measure orange juice
½ measure lime juice
3 ice cubes, crushed

to decorate
cocktail cherries
pineapple cubes
slice of orange

The name of this cocktail is taken from Tahitian and means good – it certainly is.

Dip the rim of a tall glass into the beaten egg white, then into the caster sugar. Put the rum, orange juice and lime juice into a cocktail shaker. Shake to mix. Put the ice into the glass and pour the cocktail over it. Decorate with the cherries, pineapple and a slice of orange and serve with a straw.

Serves 1

Summertime

3 ice cubes, cracked
1½ measures Grand
    Marnier or Cointreau
½ measure dark rum
2 teaspoons lemon juice
slice of lemon, to
    decorate

Both Cointreau and Grand Marnier are French liqueurs flavoured with oranges. Cointreau is a clear liquid, while Grand Marnier is brandy-based.

Put the ice cubes into a cocktail shaker and add the Grand Marnier or Cointreau, rum and lemon juice. Shake well. Strain into a cocktail glass and decorate with the slice of lemon.

Serves 1

Banana Royal

crushed ice
1½ measures coconut
    milk (see page 35)
3 measures
    pineapple juice
1½ measures golden rum
½ measure double cream
1 ripe banana
grated coconut,
    to decorate

Put some crushed ice into a blender and add the coconut milk, pineapple juice, rum, cream and banana. Blend at high speed for 15–30 seconds, until smooth and creamy. Pour into an old-fashioned glass and sprinkle with grated coconut.

Serves 1

Port Antonio

½ teaspoon grenadine
4–5 ice cubes
1 measure fresh
    lime juice
3 measures white rum or
    golden rum

to decorate
lime rind
cocktail cherry

Grenadine is a sweet non-alcoholic syrup made from pomegranates, which give it its rich rosy pink colour.

Spoon the grenadine into a chilled cocktail glass. Put the ice cubes into a mixing glass. Pour the lime juice and rum over the ice and stir vigorously, then strain into the cocktail glass. Wrap the lime rind round the cocktail cherry, spear them with a cocktail stick and use to decorate the drink.

Serves 1

St Lucia

4–5 ice cubes
1 measure Curaçao
1 measure dry vermouth
juice of ½ orange
1 teaspoon grenadine
2 measures white or
    golden rum

to decorate
orange rind spiral
cocktail cherry

Put the ice cubes into a cocktail shaker. Pour the Curaçao, dry vermouth, orange juice, grenadine and rum over the ice. Shake until a frost forms, then pour, without straining, into a highball glass. Decorate with an orange rind spiral and a cocktail cherry.

Serves 1

Bahamas

4–5 ice cubes
1 measure white rum
1 measure Southern
    Comfort
1 measure fresh
    lemon juice
1 dash crème de banane
thin lemon slice,
    to decorate

Put some ice cubes into a cocktail
shaker and pour in the rum,
Southern Comfort, lemon juice
and crème de banane. Shake
vigorously, then strain into a
chilled cocktail glass. Drop in a
thin lemon slice and serve.

Serves 1

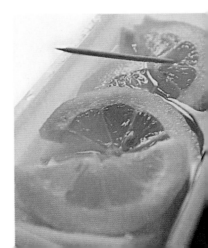

Serenade

6 ice cubes, crushed
1 measure white rum
½ measure Amaretto di
    Saronno
½ measure
    coconut cream
2 measures
    pineapple juice
slice of pineapple,
    to decorate

Amaretto is a sweet Italian liqueur made from apricot kernels, flavoured with almonds and herbs.

Put half of the ice into a blender and add the rum, Amaretto, coconut cream and pineapple juice and blend for 20 seconds. Put the remaining ice into a tall glass and pour the cocktail over it. Decorate with a slice of pineapple and drink with a straw.

Serves 1

Discovery Bay

4–5 ice cubes
3 drops Angostura bitters
juice of ½ lime
1 teaspoon Curaçao or
   blue Curaçao
1 teaspoon sugar syrup
   (see page 7)
3 measures golden or
   dark rum
lime slices, to decorate

Curaçao comes from the Dutch Caribbean island of that name. It is produced in several colours including a vivid blue and honey-gold.

Put the ice cubes into a cocktail shaker. Shake the bitters over the ice. Pour in the lime juice, Curaçao, sugar syrup and rum and shake until a frost forms. Strain into an old fashioned glass. Decorate with lime slices.

Serves 1

Pussyfoot

crushed ice
1½ measures white rum
1 measure double cream
1 measure
    pineapple juice
1 measure lime juice
1 measure cherry juice

to decorate
slice of pineapple
cocktail cherry

Although there is a well-known non-alcoholic cocktail called Pussyfoot, this more potent version, with a generous measure of rum, is something of a lion's paw.

Put some crushed ice into a blender and add the rum, cream, pineapple juice, lime juice and cherry juice. Blend at high speed for 15–20 seconds, then pour into a hurricane glass. Decorate with a slice of pineapple and a cherry.

Serves 1

Virgin's Prayer

ice

2 measures light rum

2 measures dark rum

2 measures Kahlua

2 tablespoons
    lemon juice

4 tablespoons
    orange juice

2 slices of lime, to
    decorate

Put some ice in a cocktail shaker
and pour in the rums, Kahlua,
lemon juice and orange juice and
shake until a frost forms. Strain
the cocktail into 2 rocks or
highball glasses and decorate
with the slices of lime.

Serves 2

Tip
Kahlua is a coffee
flavoured liqueur from
Mexico

54

Bombay Smash

5 ice cubes, crushed
1 measure dark rum
1 measure Malibu
3 measures
    pineapple juice
2 teaspoons lemon juice
¼ measure Cointreau

to decorate
pineapple cubes
slice of lemon

Put half of the ice into a cocktail shaker. Add the rum, Malibu, pineapple juice, lemon juice and Cointreau. Shake until a frost forms. Put the remaining ice into a tall glass and strain over the cocktail. Decorate with the pineapple cubes and slice of lemon and drink with a straw.

Serves 1

Tropical Dream

1 measure white rum
1 measure Midori
1 tablespoon coconut
     cream
1 tablespoon
     pineapple juice
3 tablespoons
     orange juice
3–4 ice cubes
½ measure crème
     de banane
½ fresh banana
wedge of fresh banana,
     with skin on,
     to decorate

Pour the white rum, Midori,
coconut cream, pineapple juice,
orange juice and the ice cubes
into a blender. Blend for about
10 seconds. Add the crème de
banane and the fresh banana and
blend for a further 10 seconds.
Decorate with the wedge of
banana and drink with a straw.

Serves 1

Punches & Fizzes

Florida Skies

cracked ice
1 measure white rum
¼ measure lime juice
½ measure
    pineapple juice
soda water, to top up
slices of cucumber or
    lime, to decorate

For a Florida Hurricane, add 1 measure Curaçao and substitute orange juice for the pineapple juice. For a Florida, add ½ measure crème de menthe and decorate with a mint sprig.

Put some cracked ice in a tall glass. Put the rum, lime and pineapple juices into a cocktail shaker. Shake lightly. Strain into the glass and top up with soda water. Decorate with the slices of cucumber or lime.

Serves 1

Havana Beach

½ lime
2 measures
    pineapple juice
1 measure white rum
1 teaspoon sugar
ginger ale, to top up
slice of lime, to decorate

A hurricane glass is so called because it is shaped like a hurricane lamp. It is ideal for long drinks.

Cut the lime into 4 pieces and place in a blender with the pineapple juice, rum and sugar. Blend until smooth. Pour into a hurricane glass or large goblet and top up with ginger ale. Decorate with a slice of lime.

Serves 1

Cuba Libre

2–3 ice cubes
1½ measures dark rum
juice of ½ lime
cola, to top up
lime slice, to decorate

Place the ice cubes in a tall tumbler and pour over the rum and lime juice. Stir to mix. Top up with cola, decorate with a lime slice and drink through a straw.

Serves 1

Mississippi Punch

crushed ice
3 drops Angostura bitters
1 teaspoon sugar syrup
(see page 7)
juice of 1 lemon
1 measure brandy
1 measure dark rum
2 measures bourbon or
Scotch whisky

Fill a highball glass with crushed ice. Shake the bitters over the ice and pour in the sugar syrup and lemon juice. Stir gently to mix thoroughly. Add the brandy, rum and whisky, in that order, stir once and serve with drinking straws.

Serves 1

Bahamas Punch

juice of 1 lemon
1 teaspoon sugar syrup
(see page 7)
3 drops Angostura bitters
½ teaspoon grenadine
3 measures white or
golden rum
slice of orange
slice of lemon
cracked ice
grated nutmeg,
to decorate

For Planter's Punch, substitute lime juice for the lemon juice, a slice of lime for the lemon slice, increase the quantity of grenadine to 1 teaspoon and use dark rum.

Pour the lemon juice and sugar syrup into a mixing glass. Shake in the bitters, then add the grenadine, rum and slices of orange and lemon. Stir thoroughly and chill in the refrigerator for 3 hours. To serve, fill an old-fashioned glass with cracked ice, pour in the punch, without straining, and sprinkle with nutmeg.

Serves 1

Pink Rum

3 drops Angostura bitters
3–4 ice cubes
2 measures white rum
2 measures
   cranberry juice
1 measure soda water
slice of lime, to decorate

Angostura bitters is a herb-flavoured essence used in small quantities to add flavour to drinks. Details of the recipe are a closely kept secret. Orange bitters are another favourite.

Shake the bitters into a highball glass and swirl them around. Add the ice cubes, then pour in the rum, cranberry juice and soda water and serve decorated with a slice of lime.

Serves 1

Tobago Fizz

4–5 ice cubes
juice of ½ lime or lemon
juice of ½ orange
3 measures golden rum
1 measure single cream
½ teaspoon sugar syrup
    (see page 7)
soda water, to top up

to decorate
slice of orange
slice of strawberry

Put the ice cubes into a cocktail shaker. Pour the lime or lemon juice, orange juice, rum, cream and sugar syrup over the ice. Shake until a frost forms, then strain into a goblet. Top with soda water and serve decorated with slices of orange and strawberry speared on a cocktail stick and drink with straws.

Serves 1

New Orleans Dandy

punches & fizzes

crushed ice
1 measure light rum
½ measure peach brandy
1 dash orange juice
1 dash lime juice
Champagne to top up

Place the crushed ice in a cocktail shaker with the rum, peach brandy, orange juice and lime juice. Shake until a frost forms. Strain into a large wine glass and top up with Champagne.

Serves 1

Pink Treasure

2 ice cubes, cracked
1 measure white rum
1 measure cherry brandy
bitter lemon or soda
    water (optional)
twist of lemon,
    to decorate

Put the ice cubes, rum and cherry brandy into a small glass. Add a splash of bitter lemon or soda water. Decorate with the twist of lemon.

Serves 1

Punch Julien

juice of 2 limes
1 measure
 pineapple juice
3 drops Angostura bitters
½ teaspoon grenadine
1 measure golden rum
3 measures dark rum
slice of lime
slice of lemon
slice of orange
cracked ice

to decorate
grated nutmeg
1 pineapple wedge

Pour the lime juice and pineapple juice into a mixing glass and shake in the bitters. Pour in the grenadine and golden and dark rums and add the fruit. Stir thoroughly, then chill in the refrigerator for 3 hours. Fill an old-fashioned glass with cracked ice. Pour the punch over the ice and add the fruit. Sprinkle with nutmeg and serve decorated with a pineapple wedge.

Serves 1

Golden Rum Punch

50 g (2 oz) sugar
1 litre (1¾ pints)
    pineapple juice
juice of 6 oranges
juice of 6 lemons
1 bottle golden rum
ice
1 litre (1¾ pints) ginger
    ale or soda water

to decorate
slices of fruit in season,
    such as pineapples,
    oranges, cherries and
    strawberries

Put the sugar into a punch bowl, pour in the pineapple juice and stir to dissolve the sugar. Add the orange and lemon juices and pour in the rum. Stir to mix. Put a large block of ice into the punch bowl and leave the punch to get really cold.

When you are ready to serve, pour in the ginger ale or soda water. Decorate with slices of pineapple and orange, cherries, strawberries and any other fruit in season.

Serves 20

Slow Sippers

Alexander Baby

Black Widow

Rum Martini

Honeysuckle

Batiste

White Witch

Heartwarmer

Between the Sheets

Sunset Tea

Island Cream Grog

Alexander Baby

4–5 ice cubes
2 measures dark rum
1 measure crème
    de cacao
½ measure double cream
grated nutmeg,
    to decorate

This is the younger – but no less powerful – brother of the classic gin- and brandy-based cocktails, Alexander and Brandy Alexander.

Put the ice cubes into a cocktail shaker and pour the rum, crème de cacao and cream over it. Shake a frost forms, then strain it into a chilled cocktail glass. Sprinkle grated nutmeg on top.

Serves 1

Tip
Crème de cacao is a chocolate-flavoured liqueur which comes in colourless and chocolate-brown varieties.

Black Widow

4–5 ice cubes
2 measures dark rum
1 measure Southern
    Comfort
juice of ½ lime
1 dash sugar syrup (see
    page 7)
slice of lime, to decorate

Put the ice cubes into a cocktail shaker. Pour in the dark rum, Southern Comfort, lime juice and sugar syrup and shake until a frost forms. Strain into a chilled cocktail glass and decorate with a slice of lime.

Serves 1

Rum Martini

slow sippers

4–5 ice cubes
1 measure dry vermouth
3 measures white rum
1 piece of lemon rind

Put the ice cubes into a mixing glass. Pour the vermouth and rum over the ice, stir vigorously, then strain into a chilled cocktail glass. Twist the lemon rind over the drink and drop it in.

Serves 1

Honeysuckle

4–5 ice cubes
2 measures golden rum
juice of 1 lime
1 teaspoon clear honey

This cocktail is especially flavoursome when made with lemon or orange blossom honey.

Put the ice cubes into a cocktail shaker. Pour in the rum and lime juice and add the honey. Shake until a frost forms, then strain into a cocktail glass.

Serves 1

Batiste

4–5 ice cubes
1 measure
  Grand Marnier
2 measures golden or
  dark rum

Grand Marnier is a brandy-based orange liqueur. It is made by a French liqueur company, hence its presence in this cocktail which comes from one of the French-speaking islands in the Caribbean.

Put the ice cubes into a mixing glass. Pour the Grand Marnier and rum over the ice, stir vigorously, then strain into a cocktail glass.

Serves 1

White Witch

8–10 ice cubes
1 measure white rum
½ measure white crème
  de cacao
½ measure Cointreau
juice of ½ lime
soda water, to top up

to decorate
slice of orange
slice of lime

Put 4–5 ice cubes into a cocktail
shaker and pour in the rum,
crème de cacao, Cointreau and
lime juice. Put 4–5 fresh ice cubes
into an old-fashioned glass.
Shake the drink, then strain it into
the glass. Top up with soda water
and stir to mix. Decorate with
slices of orange and lime and
serve with straws.

Serves 1

Tip
If you roll whole limes
around quite hard on a
board with your hand,
you will find that you get
more juice from them.

Heartwarmer

200 ml (7 fl oz) red
 grape juice
250 g (8 oz) brown sugar
350 ml (12 fl oz) dark rum
1.5 litres (2½ pints) dry
 white wine
450 ml (¾ pint) red wine

Put the grape juice into a saucepan, add the sugar and stir over a gentle heat until the sugar has dissolved completely. Stir in the dark rum and set aside. Pour the white wine and red wine into a large saucepan and heat until hot, but not boiling. Add the rum and grape juice mixture and stir together. Serve hot.

Serves 12

Between the Sheets

4–5 ice cubes
1¼ measures brandy
1 measure white rum
½ measure Cointreau
¾ measure lemon juice
½ measure sugar syrup
    (see page 7)

Put the ice cubes into a cocktail shaker. Add the brandy, white rum, Cointreau, lemon juice and sugar syrup and shake until a frost forms. Strain into a chilled cocktail glass.

Serves 1

Sunset Tea

200 ml (7 fl oz) freshly
    brewed Indian tea
½ measure golden rum
1 measure Cointreau
2 measures orange juice

to decorate
2 slices of orange, each
    stuck with 3 cloves
cinnamon sticks

Pour the tea into 2 heatproof glasses. Put the rum, Cointreau and orange juice into a small saucepan. Place it over a low heat and bring the mixture to just under boiling point, stirring constantly. Pour immediately into the glasses with the tea. Decorate with a slice of orange stuck with 3 cloves, and a cinnamon stick.

Serves 2

Island Cream Grog

2 measures rum
200 ml (7 fl oz) boiling
     water
sugar to taste
whipped cream
grated nutmeg

For Hot Buttered Rum, stir 15 g (½ oz) butter with the rum before adding the boiling water and omit the whipped cream.

Warm a heatproof glass with a handle and pour in the rum and boiling water. Add sugar to taste and stir. Spoon some whipped cream on top and sprinkle with grated nutmeg.

Serves 1

INDEX

Acknowledgements

Octopus Publishing Group
  Ltd./David Loftus 91
  /Neil Mersh 11, 13, 17, 25, 26,
  28, 39, 41, 51, 57, 58, 63,
  67, 69, 71, 75, 87
  /Peter Myers 8, 64
  /William Reavell Cover, 2, 3, 5,
  6-7, 15, 19, 20, 22, 31, 33,
  34, 37, 43, 45, 47, 48, 53,
  55, 61, 73, 77, 78, 81, 83,
  84, 89, 93, 95

TEQUILA

TEQUILA

spruce

An Hachette UK Company
www.hachette.co.uk

First published in Great Britain in 2014 by
Spruce, a division of Octopus Publishing Group Ltd
Carmelite House, 50 Victoria Embankment, London EC4Y 0DZ
www.octopusbooks.co.uk
www.octopusbooksusa.com

This edition published in 2018.

Copyright © Octopus Publishing Group Ltd 2014, 2018

Distributed in the US by Hachette Book Group
1290 Avenue of the Americas, 4th and 5th Floors, New York, NY 10104

Distributed in Canada by Canadian Manda Group
664 Annette Street, Toronto, Ontario, Canada M6S 2C8

These recipes have previously been published by Hamlyn.

ISBN 978-1-84601-574-8

A CIP catalogue record for this book is available from the British Library

Printed and bound in China

10 9 8 7 6 5 4 3 2 1

Notes for American readers: The measure that has been used in the recipes is based on a bar jigger, which is 45 ml (1½ fl oz). If preferred, a different volume can be used providing the proportions are kept constant within a drink and suitable adjustments are made to spoon measurements, where they occur.
Standard level spoon measurements are used in all recipes: 1 tablespoon = one 15 ml spoon. 1 teaspoon = one 5 ml spoon. Imperial and metric measurements have been given in some of the recipes. Use one set of measurements only and not a mixture of both.

UK	US
caster sugar	granulated sugar
cocktail cherries	maraschino cherries
cocktail stick	toothpick
double cream	heavy cream
drinking chocolate	presweetened cocoa powder
icing sugar	confectioners' sugar
jug	pitcher
lemon rind	lemon peel or zest
single cream	light cream
soda water	club soda

Contents

Introduction

Tequila has a bizarre and exotic quality that is missing from the other major spirits. Distilled from the root of the maguey or blue agave, a cactus-like plant which actually belongs to the amaryllis family, it is Mexico's contribution to the great drinks of the world.

Pulque was the first drink to be produced from the agave. It is made by fermenting the sap from the plant, and dates back to prehispanic times. A low alcohol drink, it is still drunk today. When the Spaniards conquered Mexico in 1519–21, one of the many things they introduced was the art of distilling and they turned their attention to pulque. During the late 18th and early 19th century it was realized that the best *aguardiente de agave*, as the distilled spirit was known, was produced around the town of Tequila in the state of Jalisco.

By the late 19th century the commercial cultivation of agaves in Mexico had begun and by the 1870s there were about a dozen distilleries. The United States was the first, and is still the most important export market for tequila, but it was not until the mid-sixties that tequila burst upon the rest of the world. By the seventies the demand had led to a need for regulations to define tequila and to protect the name, limiting its production to tequila produced in the state of Jalisco.

Tequila has been described as having a smooth sharpness. There are several types. Tequila blanco, the original version, is colourless while tequila reposado (gold) is aged in oak barrels for up to 11 months. Tequila añejo has longer ageing. Mezcal is an another agave-distilled spirit but with a different style from tequila.

Mezcals labelled 'con gusano' contain a worm. Despite widespread belief, tequila does not contain a worm.

The traditional way to drink tequila is with a pinch of salt. The practice is to lick the salt from between the thumb and forefinger, then knock back the tequila from a shot glass and suck a wedge of lime or lemon. As a variation, sips from a glass of tequila may be alternated with sips of sangrita, a highly spiced tomato juice. Salt is also used for rimming the glass of the Margarita, a delicious concoction of tequila, Cointreau and fresh lime juice and the most famous tequila cocktail of all. It originated in the late thirties at the hotel bar in the Rancho la Gloria, Rosarita Beach, Tijuana, where it was thought to be created by Danny Herrera for the actress Marjorie King, who was allergic to all spirits except tequila. He named it Margarita – the Spanish for Marjorie.

Bar Equipment
Cocktails are all the better for being made correctly. A well-stocked home bar should contain the following equipment: a cocktail shaker for drinks which are shaken, a mixing glass (also called a bar glass) and a long-handled bar spoon for drinks that are stirred rather than shaken, and a blender for making drinks with ingredients such as fresh fruit and egg white. A set of bar measures; a canelle knife for removing spirals of lime, lemon and orange rind; a lemon squeezer; ice containers and tongs for lifting ice cubes; and a salt saucer for rimming glasses are all important for tequila cocktails, as are a chopping board and a sharp knife.

Sugar Syrup
Using sugar syrup is the most practical way of sweetening a drink. Since the sugar is already dissolved it does not need lengthy stirring to blend it into a cold drink. Pour equal quantities of sugar and water (6 tablespoons of each is a practical amount) into a small saucepan and bring to the boil, stirring to dissolve the sugar, then boil for 1–2 minutes without stirring. Sugar syrup can be stored in the refrigerator in a sterilized bottle for up to 2 months.

Strictly Margaritas

Original Margarita

Floreciente

Cadillac

Pink Cadillac Convertible

Cobalt Margarita

Playa del Mar

Ruby Rita

Forest Fruit

Maracuja

Original
Margarita

3 lime wedges
fine sea salt
1¼ measures tequila
¾ measure Cointreau
1¼ measures fresh
    lime juice
4–5 ice cubes
lime wheel, to decorate

Dampen the rim of a chilled cocktail glass with 1 of the lime wedges then dip the rim into fine sea salt. Pour the tequila, Cointreau and lime juice into a cocktail shaker. Squeeze the juice from the remaining 2 lime wedges into the shaker, squeeze the wedges to release the oils in the skin then drop the wedges into the shaker. Add the ice cubes and shake vigorously for about 10 seconds. Strain the cocktail into the chilled glass and decorate with a lime wheel.

Serves 1

Floreciente

1 orange slice
fine sea salt
crushed ice
1¼ measures tequila gold
¾ measure Cointreau
¾ measure fresh
    lemon juice
¾ measure fresh blood
    orange juice
blood orange wedge, to
    decorate

Dampen the rim of a 300 ml
(½ pint) old-fashioned glass with
an orange slice then dip the glass
into fine sea salt and fill it with
crushed ice. Pour the tequila,
Cointreau, lemon juice and blood
orange juice into a cocktail
shaker, shake vigorously for
10 seconds then strain into the
old-fashioned glass. Decorate
with a blood orange wedge.

Serves 1

Cadillac

3 lime wedges
fine sea salt
4–5 ice cubes
1¼ measures tequila gold
½ measure Cointreau
1¼ measures fresh
    lime juice
2 teaspoons Grand
    Marnier
lime slice, to decorate

Dampen the rim of a chilled cocktail glass with 1 of the lime wedges, then dip the rim into fine sea salt. Pour the tequila, Cointreau and lime juice into a cocktail shaker. Squeeze the juice from the 2 remaining lime wedges into the shaker, pressing the rind to release its oils. Drop the wedges into the shaker. Add the ice cubes and shake vigorously for 10 seconds then strain the drink into the glass. Drizzle the Grand Marnier over the top of the drink. Decorate with a lime slice.

Serves 1

12

Pink Cadillac Convertible

3 lime wedges
fine sea salt
ice cubes
1¼ measures tequila gold
½ measure Cointreau
¾ measure fresh
   lime juice
¾ measure cranberry
   juice
lime wedge, to decorate
¾ measure Grand
   Marnier

Dampen the rim of a 300 ml (½ pint) old-fashioned glass with 1 of the lime wedges, then dip the rim into fine sea salt and fill the glass with ice cubes. Pour the tequila, Cointreau, lime juice and cranberry juice into a cocktail shaker. Squeeze the juice from the 2 remaining lime wedges into the shaker, pressing the rind to release its oils. Drop the wedges into the shaker. Add 4–5 ice cubes and shake vigorously for 10 seconds then strain the drink into the glass. Decorate with a lime wedge. Pour the Grand Marnier into a shot glass and serve it on the side. This should be poured on to the top of the cocktail just before drinking.

Serves 1

Cobalt Margarita

1 lime wedge
fine sea salt
1¼ measures tequila
2 teaspoons Cointreau
½ measure blue Curaçao
¾ measure fresh
    lime juice
¾ measure fresh
    grapefruit juice
4–5 ice cubes
lime rind spiral, to
    decorate

Dampen the rim of a chilled cocktail glass with a lime wedge then dip it into fine sea salt. Pour the tequila, Cointreau, blue Curaçao, lime juice and grapefruit juice into a cocktail shaker. Add the ice cubes and shake vigorously for 10 seconds then strain into the cocktail glass. Decorate with a lime rind spiral.

Serves 1

Tip
To make a citrus spiral, pare the rind from the fruit with a canelle knife or vegetable peeler then wind it tightly round a glass swizzle stick.

Playa del Mar

1 orange slice
light brown sugar and
    sea salt mixture
ice cubes
1¼ measures tequila gold
¾ measure Grand
    Marnier
2 teaspoons fresh
    lime juice
¾ measure cranberry
    juice
¾ measure fresh
    pineapple juice

to decorate
pineapple wedge
orange rind spiral

Dampen the rim of a sling glass
with the orange slice then dip
it into the brown sugar and sea
salt mixture. Fill the glass with
ice cubes. Pour the tequila,
Grand Marnier, lime juice,
cranberry juice and pineapple
juice into a cocktail shaker. Fill
the shaker with ice cubes and
shake vigorously for 10 seconds
then strain into the sling glass.
Decorate with a pineapple wedge
and an orange rind spiral.

Serves 1

Ruby Rita

1¼ measures fresh pink
    grapefruit juice
fine sea salt
ice cubes
1¼ measures tequila gold
¾ measure Cointreau
pink grapefruit wedge, to
    decorate

Dampen the rim of 300 ml
(½ pint) old-fashioned glass with
some pink grapefruit juice and
dip it into fine sea salt. Fill the
glass with ice cubes. Pour the
tequila, Cointreau and pink
grapefruit juice into a cocktail
shaker, fill with more ice and
shake vigorously. Strain into the
old-fashioned glass and decorate
with a pink grapefruit wedge.

Serves 1

Forest Fruit

1 lime wedge
brown sugar
2 blackberries
2 raspberries
2 teaspoons Chambord
2 teaspoons Crème
de Mure
1¼ measures tequila
2 teaspoons Cointreau
1¼ measures fresh
lemon juice
crushed ice

to decorate
lemon slices
blackberry
raspberry

Chambord is a black raspberry liqueur and Crème de Mure is a blackberry one.

Dampen the rim of an old-fashioned glass with a lime wedge and dip it into brown sugar. Drop the blackberries and raspberries into the glass and muddle to a pulp with the back of a spoon or a porcelain pestle. Stir in the Chambord and Crème de Mure. Pour in the tequila, Cointreau and lemon juice, fill with crushed ice and stir gently, lifting the muddled berries from the bottom of the glass. Decorate with lemon slices, a blackberry and a raspberry.

Serves 1

Maracuja

1 fresh ripe passion fruit
1¼ measures tequila gold
1 tablespoon Creole
    Shrub
¾ measure fresh
    lime juice
2 teaspoons Cointreau
1 teaspoon passion
    fruit syrup
4–5 ice cubes
physalis (Cape
    gooseberry), to
    decorate

Creole Shrub is a golden-coloured rum, flavoured with orange peel.

Cut the passion fruit in half and scoop the flesh into a cocktail shaker. Add the tequila, Creole Shrub, lime juice, Cointreau, passion fruit syrup and ice cubes and shake vigorously for 10 seconds. Strain through a small fine sieve into a chilled cocktail glass. Decorate with a physalis.

Serves 1

Tip

It is important to use a really ripe passion fruit for this drink.

Cool
Classics

South of the Border

Alleluia

Mezcarita

Tequini

Sour Apple

Chapala

Ananas e Coco

Honey Water

Bloody Maria

Frozen Strawberry

Japanese Slipper

Mockingbird

Pancho Villa

Coco Loco

Tequila Sunset

South of the Border

1¼ measures tequila
¾ measure Kahlúa
1¼ measures fresh
    lime juice
4–5 ice cubes

to decorate
lime wedge
brown sugar
ground coffee

Kahlúa is as Mexican as tequila. It is a liqueur made from Mexican coffee beans.

Pour the tequila, Kahlúa and lime juice into a cocktail shaker. Add the ice cubes and shake vigorously for 10 seconds then strain into a chilled cocktail glass. To decorate, take a lime wedge, press one side into a saucer of sugar and the other side into a saucer of ground coffee, and serve on the side.

Serves 1

Alleluia

¾ measure tequila
½ measure blue Curaçao
2 teaspoons
    maraschino syrup
dash of egg white
¾ measure fresh
    lemon juice
ice cubes
100 ml (3½ fl oz)
    bitter lemon

to decorate
lemon slice
maraschino cherry
mint sprig

Pour the tequila, blue Curaçao, maraschino syrup, egg white and lemon juice into a cocktail shaker, add 4–5 ice cubes and shake vigorously. Fill a 350 ml (12 fl oz) highball glass with ice cubes and strain the drink over the ice. Top up with the bitter lemon and stir gently. Decorate with a lemon slice, cherry and mint sprig.

Serves 1

Tip
For maraschino syrup, use the syrup from the jar of maraschino cherries.

Mezcarita

1 lemon wedge
chilli salt
1¼ measures mezcal
¾ measure Cointreau
1¼ measures fresh
    lemon juice
4–5 ice cubes
lemon rind spiral, to
    decorate

Dampen the rim of a chilled
cocktail glass with the wedge of
lemon and dip it into chilli salt.
Pour the mezcal, Cointreau and
lemon juice into a cocktail shaker,
add the ice cubes and shake
vigorously. Strain into the
cocktail glass and decorate with
the lemon rind spiral.

Serves 1

Tequini

ice cubes
3 dashes orange bitters
75 ml (3 fl oz) tequila
   blanco
2 teaspoons dry French
   vermouth, preferably
   Noilly Prat
black olive, to decorate

This is the Mexican equivalent of a martini, with tequila replacing the gin and the orange bitters adding an exotic tang. It is one of the few drinks decorated with a black olive rather than a green one.

Fill a mixing glass with ice cubes then add the orange bitters and tequila. Stir gently with a bar spoon for 10 seconds. Take a chilled cocktail glass and add the vermouth, film the inside of the glass with the vermouth then tip it out. Stir the bitters and tequila for a further 10 seconds and strain into the chilled glass. Decorate with a large black olive.

Serves 1

Sour Apple

1¼ measures tequila
2 teaspoons Cointreau
1 tablespoon apple
  schnapps
¾ measure fresh
  lime juice
¾ measure dry
  apple juice
4–5 ice cubes
wedge of Granny Smith
  apple, to decorate

Pour the tequila, Cointreau, apple schnapps, lime juice and apple juice into a cocktail shaker, add the ice cubes and shake vigorously for 10 seconds then strain into a chilled cocktail glass. Decorate with a Granny Smith apple wedge.

Serves 1

Chapala

1¼ measures tequila
¾ measure Cointreau
¾ measure fresh
    lemon juice
¾ measure fresh
    orange juice
2 teaspoons grenadine
orange rind spiral, to
    decorate

Pour the tequila, Cointreau,
lemon juice and orange juice
into a cocktail shaker. Add the
grenadine and shake vigorously
for 10 seconds then strain into a
chilled cocktail glass. Decorate
with an orange rind spiral.

Serves 1

Ananas & Coco

1¼ measures tequila gold
¾ measure coconut syrup
1 large chunk fresh
    pineapple
1¼ measures pineapple
    juice
crushed ice
pineapple wedge, to
    decorate

Put the tequila, coconut syrup,
pineapple chunk and pineapple
juice into a blender. Add a
handful of crushed ice, blend
for 20 seconds then pour into a
wine goblet. Decorate with a
pineapple wedge.

Serves 1

Honey Water

4–5 ice cubes
1¼ measures tequila gold
¾ measure sweet
   vermouth
3 dashes Angostura
   bitters
3 dashes Peychaud
   bitters
2 teaspoons Grand
   Marnier

to decorate
maraschino cherry
orange rind spiral

Put the ice cubes into a mixing glass, pour in the tequila, vermouth and both bitters and stir gently for 10 seconds. Put the Grand Marnier into a chilled cocktail glass, film the inside of the glass with the Grand Marnier then tip it out. Stir the contents of the mixing glass again for 10 seconds then strain into the cocktail glass. Decorate with a maraschino cherry and an orange rind spiral.

Serves 1

Bloody Maria

1 lime wedge
celery salt
black pepper
ice cubes
1¼ measures tequila
2 teaspoons medium
   sherry
2 dashes Tabasco sauce
4 dashes Worcestershire
   sauce
1 tablespoon fresh
   lime juice
100 ml (3½ fl oz) fresh
   tomato juice
cayenne pepper
4–5 ice cubes

to decorate
celery stick
lime wedge
basil sprig

Dampen the rim of a 350 ml
(12 fl oz) old-fashioned glass with
a lime wedge then dip it into
celery salt and black pepper. Fill
a cocktail shaker with ice cubes
then add the tequila, sherry,
Tabasco sauce, Worcestershire
sauce, lime juice, tomato juice
and a pinch each of celery salt,
black pepper and cayenne
pepper. Add the ice cubes and
shake vigorously then pour into
the old-fashioned glass. Decorate
with the celery stick, lime wedge
and a basil sprig.

Serves 1

Frozen
Strawberry

sugar
a small handful of
    crushed ice
2 measures tequila
1 measure strawberry
    liqueur
1 measure fresh
    lime juice
4 ripe strawberries
1 teaspoon Sugar Syrup
    (see page 7)
fresh strawberry,
    unhulled, to decorate

Dampen the rim of a chilled
cocktail glass and dip it into the
sugar. Put the crushed ice into a
blender and pour in the tequila,
strawberry liqueur and lime
juice. Drop in the strawberries,
add the sugar syrup and blend
for a few seconds. Pour without
straining into a cocktail glass and
decorate with a strawberry.

Serves 1

Japanese Slipper

1 lime wedge
brown sugar
1¼ measures tequila
¾ measure Midori
1¼ measures fresh
   lime juice
4–5 ice cubes
lime wedge, to decorate

Midori is a Japanese melon liqueur. Combined with tequila and lime juice, it makes a delectable drink.

Dampen the rim of a chilled cocktail glass with a lime wedge then dip the rim into brown sugar. Pour the tequila, Midori and lime juice into a cocktail shaker and add the ice cubes. Shake vigorously for about 10 seconds then strain into the cocktail glass and decorate with a lime wedge.

Serves 1

Mockingbird

1¼ measures tequila
¾ measure green Crème
de Menthe
1¼ measures fresh
lime juice
4–5 ice cubes
lemon rind spiral, to
decorate

Pour the tequila, crème de menthe and lime juice into a cocktail shaker. Add the ice cubes, shake vigorously for about 10 seconds then strain into a chilled cocktail glass. Decorate with a lemon rind spiral.

Serves 1

Pancho Villa

1 measure tequila
½ measure Tia Maria
1 teaspoon Cointreau
4–5 ice cubes
brandied cherry, to
    decorate (optional)

Pour the tequila, Tia Maria
and Cointreau into a cocktail
shaker. Add the ice cubes, shake
vigorously for about 10 seconds,
then strain into a cocktail glass.
Decorate with a brandied cherry,
if liked.

Serves 1

Coco Loco

¾ measure white rum
¾ measure tequila
½ measure vodka
1 measure coconut
    cream
2 measures fresh
    lemon juice
3 ice cubes, cracked

to decorate
lemon rind twist
cocktail cherries

Pour the rum, tequila, vodka, coconut cream and lemon juice into a blender. Mix for 15 seconds. Put the ice cubes into a large goblet and pour over the drink. Decorate with the lemon rind twist and cherries and drink with a straw.

Serves 1

Tequila Sunset

1 measure tequila gold
1 measure fresh
   lemon juice
1 measure fresh
   orange juice
1 tablespoon honey
crushed ice
lemon rind spiral, to
   decorate

Put the tequila into a chilled cocktail glass, add the lemon juice and then the orange juice and stir. Drizzle the honey into the glass so that it falls in a layer to the bottom, add the crushed ice and decorate with a lemon rind spiral.

Serves 1

Long Shots

Texas Tea

Matador

Mexicola

Tijuana Sling

Rosarita Bay Breeze

El Diablo

Agave Julep

Sunburn

Gold Digger

Tequila Sunrise

Rooster Booster

Mexicana

Thai Sunrise

Pepper Eater

Baja Sour

Brooklyn Bomber

Tequila de Coco

Jalisco Swizzle

Acapulco

Desert Daisy

Long Island Iced Tea

Texas Tea

¾ measure tequila
1 tablespoon white rum
1 tablespoon Cointreau
2 teaspoons Sugar Syrup
    (see page 7)
¾ measure fresh
    lemon juice
¾ measure fresh
    orange juice
100 ml (3½ fl oz) strong
    fruit tea, chilled
ice cubes

to decorate
orange slice
lemon slice
mint sprig

Pour the tequila, rum, Cointreau, sugar syrup, lemon juice, orange juice and tea into a cocktail shaker, add a handful of ice cubes and shake vigorously. Fill a 350 ml (12 fl oz) sling glass with fresh ice cubes and strain the drink over them. Decorate with orange and lemon slices and a mint sprig.

Serves 1

Tip

One of the best teas to use as a base for this refreshing drink is a mixed berry tea. Its essential fruitiness blends very well with the citrus juices in Texas Tea.

Matador

1¼ measures tequila
¾ measure fresh
    lime juice
100 ml (3½ fl oz)
    pineapple juice
1 pineapple chunk
2 teaspoons Sugar Syrup
    (see page 7)
crushed ice

to decorate
pineapple wedge
lime rind spiral

Put the tequila, lime juice,
pineapple juice, pineapple chunk
and sugar syrup into a blender.
Add a handful of crushed ice and
blend for 15 seconds. Pour into a
highball glass and decorate with
a pineapple wedge and a lime
rind spiral.

Serves 1

Mexicola

4 lime wedges
crushed ice
1¼ measures tequila
150 ml (¼ pint) Coca-Cola

Put the lime wedges into a
350 ml (12 fl oz) highball glass
and crush gently with a pestle to
release the juices and oils. Fill the
glass with crushed ice, then pour
in the tequila and Coca-Cola. Stir
gently lifting the lime wedges
through the drink.

Serves 1

Tijuana Sling

1¼ measures tequila
¾ measure crème
   de cassis
¾ measure fresh
   lime juice
2 dashes Peychaud
   bitters
4–5 ice cubes
100 ml (3½ fl oz)
   ginger ale

to decorate
lime wheel
fresh blackcurrants or
   blueberries

Pour the tequila, crème de cassis, lime juice and Peychaud bitters into a cocktail shaker. Add the ice cubes and shake vigorously. Pour into a 350 ml (12 fl oz) sling glass then top up with ginger ale. Decorate with a lime wheel and fresh berries.

Serves 1

Rosarita Bay Breeze

ice cubes
1¼ measures tequila
150 ml (¼ pint) cranberry
    juice
1¼ measures pineapple
    juice
orange slice, to decorate

Put the ice cubes into a 350 ml (12 fl oz) highball glass and pour in the tequila and cranberry juice. Float the pineapple juice over the top of the drink and decorate with an orange slice.

Serves 1

El Diablo

ice cubes
1¼ measures tequila gold
¾ measure fresh
    lime juice
2 teaspoons grenadine
100 ml (3½ fl oz)
    ginger ale
lime slice, to decorate

Fill a 350 ml (12 fl oz) highball glass with ice cubes, then pour in the tequila, lime juice and grenadine. Top up with ginger ale and stir gently. Decorate with a lime slice.

Serves 1

Agave Julep

8 torn mint leaves
1 tablespoon Sugar
   Syrup (see page 7)
1¼ measures tequila gold
1¼ measures fresh
   lime juice
crushed ice

to decorate
lime wedge
mint sprig

Put the mint leaves into a 350 ml (12 fl oz) highball glass and cover with sugar syrup. Muddle with a pestle to release the mint oils. Add the tequila and lime juice, fill the glass with crushed ice and stir vigorously. Decorate with a lime wedge and a mint sprig.

Serves 1

Sunburn

ice cubes
¾ measure tequila gold
1 tablespoon Cointreau
150 ml (¼ pint) cranberry
    juice
orange slice, to decorate

Fill a 350 ml (12 fl oz) highball glass with ice cubes, then pour in the tequila, Cointreau and cranberry juice. Decorate with an orange slice.

Serves 1

Tip

Decorative ice cubes make an unusual finishing touch for drinks. Half-fill an ice cube tray with water and freeze until firm. Prepare pieces of citrus rind or mint sprigs and dip into cold water. Add to the ice tray and freeze again. Top up with water and freeze until firm.

Gold Digger

ice cubes
¾ measure tequila gold
¾ measure golden rum
150 ml (¼ pint) fresh
    orange juice
2 teaspoons Grand
    Marnier
orange slice, to decorate

Put some ice cubes into a 350 ml (12 fl oz) highball glass. Pour in the tequila, rum and orange juice and stir gently. Drizzle over the Grand Marnier and decorate with an orange slice.

Serves 1

Tequila Sunrise

5–6 ice cubes
1 measure tequila
100 ml (3½ fl oz) fresh
    orange juice
2 teaspoons grenadine

to decorate
star fruit slice
orange slice

The Tequila Sunrise is one of the cocktails which was popular during the Prohibition years in the United States, when the orange juice helped to disguise the unpleasant taste of raw alcohol.

Crack half the ice cubes and put them into a cocktail shaker. Add the tequila and orange juice and shake to mix. Put the remaining ice into a tall glass and strain the tequila into it. Slowly pour in the grenadine and allow it to settle. Just before serving, stir once. Decorate the glass with the star fruit and orange slice.

Serves 1

Rooster Booster

ice cubes
1¼ measures tequila
150 ml (¼ pint) fresh
    grapefruit juice
1 tablespoon grenadine
100 ml (3½ fl oz) soda
    water

to decorate
lime wheel
maraschino cherry

Put some ice cubes into a 350 ml (12 fl oz) highball glass. Pour in the tequila, grapefruit juice and grenadine, stir gently then top up with soda water. Decorate with a lime wheel and a cherry.

Serves 1

Mexicana

8–10 ice cubes
1¼ measures tequila
¾ measure Framboise
¾ measure fresh
    lemon juice
100 ml (3½ fl oz)
    pineapple juice

to decorate
pineapple wedge
lemon slice

Framboise is an alcool blanc, a fruit liqueur (in this case a raspberry one) which is stored in glass rather than wood and so does not acquire any colour from the cask while it matures.

Put 4–5 ice cubes into a 350 ml (12 fl oz) highball glass. Pour the tequila, Framboise, lemon juice and pineapple juice into a cocktail shaker. Add 4–5 ice cubes and shake vigorously for about 10 seconds. Pour into the highball glass and decorate with a pineapple wedge and a lemon slice.

Serves 1

Thai Sunrise

½ ripe mango, peeled and
    sliced
¾ measure tequila
1 tablespoon Cointreau
1 teaspoon grenadine
¾ measure fresh lime or
    lemon juice
¾ measure Sugar Syrup
    (see page 7)
2–3 ice cubes, cracked
lime slices, to decorate

Put all the ingredients into a
food processor and blend until
the ice is crushed. Pour into an
old-fashioned glass and decorate
with lime slices.

Serves 1

Pepper Eater

ice cubes
1¼ measures tequila
¾ measure Cointreau
100 ml (3½ fl oz)
    cranberry juice
1¼ measures fresh
    orange juice
orange slice, to decorate

Fill a 350 ml (12 fl oz) glass with ice cubes. Pour in the tequila, Cointreau, cranberry juice and orange juice and stir gently. Decorate with an orange slice.

Serves 1

Tip
Rolling an orange or any other citrus fruit hard on a board before you squeeze it helps extract more juice.

Baja Sour

1¼ measures tequila gold
2 teaspoons Sugar Syrup
    (see page 7)
1¼ measures fresh
    lemon juice
2 dashes orange bitters
½ egg white
4–5 ice cubes
1 tablespoon amontillado
    sherry

Pour the tequila, sugar syrup, lemon juice, orange bitters and egg white into a cocktail shaker. Add 4–5 ice cubes and shake vigorously. Pour into a 300 ml (½ pint) sour glass and drizzle over the sherry. Decorate with lemon slices and an orange rind spiral.

Serves 1

to decorate
lemon slices
orange rind spiral

Brooklyn Bomber

5 ice cubes, crushed
1 measure tequila
½ measure Cointreau
½ measure cherry brandy
½ measure Galliano
1 measure lemon juice

to decorate
orange wheel
cocktail cherry

Put half the ice cubes into a
cocktail shaker and add the
tequila, Cointreau, cherry brandy,
Galliano and lemon juice. Shake
to mix. Put the remaining ice
into a tall glass and pour over
the drink. Decorate with the
orange slice and cherry and
serve with straws.

Serves 1

Tip
To make crushed ice, put
some ice cubes into a
strong polythene bag,
seal it tightly, then hit it
with a rolling pin to break
up the ice.

Tequila de Coco

small handful of
   crushed ice
1 measure tequila
1 measure fresh
   lemon juice
1 measure coconut syrup
3 dashes maraschino
lemon slice, to decorate

Put the crushed ice into a blender
and add the tequila, lemon juice,
coconut syrup and maraschino.
Blend for a few seconds then
pour into a Collins glass and
decorate with a lemon slice.

Serves 1

Jalisco Swizzle

crushed ice
3 dashes Angostura
    bitters
¾ measure tequila gold
¾ measure golden rum
1¼ measures fresh
    lime juice
¾ measure passion
    fruit juice
2 teaspoons Sugar Syrup
    (see page 7)
4–5 ice cubes
¾ measure soda water

to decorate
lime wheel
mint sprig

Fill a chilled 350 ml (12 fl oz)
highball glass with crushed ice.
Put the Angostura into a cocktail
shaker, pour in the tequila, rum,
lime juice, passion fruit juice and
sugar syrup. Add the ice cubes
and shake vigorously then strain
into the highball glass. Top up
with soda and stir briefly until the
glass frosts. Decorate with a lime
wheel and a mint sprig.

Serves 1

Acapulco

cracked ice
1 measure tequila
1 measure white rum
2 measures pineapple
    juice
1 measure fresh
    grapefruit juice
1 measure coconut syrup
ice cubes
pineapple wedge, to
    decorate

Put some cracked ice into a cocktail shaker and pour in the tequila, rum, pineapple juice, grapefruit juice and coconut syrup. Fill a tall glass with ice cubes. Shake the drink and pour it over the ice. Decorate with a pineapple wedge and serve with straws.

Serves 1

Tip
Fruit syrups can be bought in good off-licenses, department stores or coffee shops.

Desert Daisy

crushed ice
1 measure tequila
1¼ measures fresh
    lime juice
2 teaspoons Sugar Syrup
    (see page 7)
1 tablespoon Fraise
    de Bois

to decorate
blackberry
strawberry
lime wedge
orange wedge
mint sprig

Half fill a 350 ml (12 fl oz) old-fashioned glass with crushed ice. Pour in the tequila, lime juice and sugar syrup and stir gently until the glass frosts. Add more crushed ice then float the Fraise de Bois on top. Decorate with a blackberry, a strawberry, a lime wedge, orange wedge and a mint sprig.

Serves 1

Long Island Iced Tea

½ measure gin
½ measure vodka
½ measure white rum
½ measure tequila
½ measure Cointreau
¾ measure lemon juice
½ teaspoon Sugar Syrup
   (see page 7)
ice cubes
Coca-Cola

to decorate
lemon slices
mint sprigs

Long Island Iced Tea was popular during the Eighties. A highly intoxicating blend of colourless spirits and Coca-Cola, it really does look like iced tea.

Pour the gin, vodka, rum, tequila, Cointreau, lemon juice and sugar syrup into a mixing glass and stir thoroughly. Fill a tall glass almost full with ice cubes then strain the drink into it. Top up with Coca-Cola and decorate with lemon slices and mint sprigs.

Serves 1

Creamy & Exotic Cocktails

Silk Stocking

Brave Bull

Sombrero

Acapulco Bliss

Mexican Bulldog

Frostbite

Silk Stocking

drinking chocolate
   powder
¾ measure tequila
¾ measure white Crème
   de Cacao
100 ml (3½ fl oz) single
   cream
2 teaspoons grenadine
4–5 ice cubes

Dampen the rim of a chilled
cocktail glass and dip it into the
drinking chocolate powder. Pour
the tequila, white Crème de
Cacao, cream and grenadine into
a cocktail shaker and add the ice
cubes. Shake vigorously for
10 seconds then strain into the
chilled cocktail glass.

Serves 1

Brave Bull

ice cubes
¾ measure tequila
¾ measure Kahlúa

Fill an old-fashioned glass with ice cubes, pour in the tequila and Kahlúa and stir gently.

Serves 1

Variations

BROWN COW

To turn a Brave Bull into a Brown Cow, add 1¼ measures single cream and stir to blend it in.

RAGING BULL

To turn a Brave Bull into a Raging Bull, add 1 teaspoon flaming Sambucca.

Sombrero

¾ measure tequila gold
¾ measure dark Crème
    de Cacao
100 ml (3½ fl oz) single
    cream
4–5 ice cubes
grated nutmeg, to
    decorate

Pour the tequila, Crème de Cacao and cream into a cocktail shaker. Add the ice cubes and shake vigorously for 10 seconds then strain into a chilled cocktail glass. To decorate, sprinkle the top of the drink with grated nutmeg.

Serves 1

Tip
Crème de Cacao, the chocolate liqueur, comes in two versions, dark and white. Choose according to how you want your drink to look. Combining the dark version in a Sombrero with tequila gold and cream results in a subtle coffee-coloured drink.

Acapulco Bliss

¾ measure tequila
1 tablespoon Pisang
  Ambon (banana
  liqueur)
2 teaspoons Galliano
¾ measure fresh
  lemon juice
¾ measure single cream
100 ml (3½ fl oz) passion
  fruit juice
4–5 ice cubes

to decorate
lemon slices
pineapple wedge
mint sprig

Pour the tequila, Pisang Ambon, Galliano, lemon juice, cream and passion fruit juice into a cocktail shaker, add the ice cubes and shake vigorously. Pour into a 350 ml (12 fl oz) sling glass and decorate with lemon slices, a pineapple wedge and a mint sprig.

Serves 1

Mexican Bulldog

ice cubes
¾ measure tequila
¾ measure Kahlúa
1¼ measures single
    cream
100 ml (3½ fl oz)
    Coca-Cola
drinking chocolate
    powder, to decorate

Put some ice cubes into a
375 g (12 oz) highball glass. Pour
in the tequila, Kahlúa and cream
then top up with Coca-Cola. Stir
gently and serve decorated with
drinking chocolate powder.

Serves 1

Frostbite

4–5 ice cubes
1 measure tequila
1 measure double cream
1 measure white Crème
    de Cacao
½ measure white Crème
    de Menthe
drinking chocolate
    powder, to decorate

Put the ice cubes into a cocktail shaker. Pour in the tequila, cream, Crème de Cacao, and Crème de Menthe and shake vigorously for 10 seconds. Strain into a chilled cocktail glass and sprinkle with drinking chocolate powder.

Serves 1

INDEX

Photography by
    William Reavell
Cocktails written and styled
by Wayne Collins at
19:20, 19–20 Great
Sutton Street, London
EC1V 0DR

Acknowledgements

Octopus Publishing Group Ltd./
Neil Mersh 10/ Peter
Myers/ Neil Mersh 49, 75/
William Reavell Cover, 2,
3, 5, 6–8, 11–16, 19–21,
23, 25, 26, 28, 31, 33, 34,
37, 39, 40, 43, 45, 47, 51,
52, 55, 57–59, 61–63, 65,
67, 68, 71, 73, 76, 79, 81,
82, 84, 87, 89–91, 93, 94

GIN

GIN

spruce

An Hachette UK Company
www.hachette.co.uk

First published in Great Britain in 2014 by
Spruce, a division of Octopus Publishing Group Ltd
Carmelite House, 50 Victoria Embankment, London EC4Y 0DZ
www.octopusbooks.co.uk
www.octopusbooksusa.com

This edition published in 2018.

Distributed in the US by Hachette Book Group
1290 Avenue of the Americas, 4th and 5th Floors, New York, NY 10104

Distributed in Canada by Canadian Manda Group
664 Annette Street, Toronto, Ontario, Canada M6S 2C8

These recipes have previously been published by Hamlyn.

ISBN 978-1-84601-574-8

A CIP catalogue record for this book is available from the British Library

Printed and bound in China

10 9 8 7 6 5 4 3 2 1

Notes for American readers: The measure that has been used in the recipes is based on a
bar jigger, which is 45 ml (1½ fl oz). If preferred, a different volume can be used providing the
proportions are kept constant within a drink and suitable adjustments are made to spoon
measurements, where they occur.
Standard level spoon measurements are used in all recipes: 1 tablespoon = one 15 ml spoon.
1 teaspoon = one 5 ml spoon. Imperial and metric measurements have been given in some
of the recipes. Use one set of measurements only and not a mixture of both.

UK	US
caster sugar	granulated sugar
cocktail cherries	maraschino cherries
cocktail stick	toothpick
double cream	heavy cream
drinking chocolate	presweetened cocoa powder
icing sugar	confectioners' sugar
jug	pitcher
lemon rind	lemon peel or zest
single cream	light cream
soda water	club soda

Contents

Introduction

Gin is a clear grain spirit, further distilled with a variety of herb and fruit flavourings – the botanicals – which has been produced commercially for over 400 years. Originally from Holland, it has had a chequered social career, sinking to the lowest social depths in 18th-century London, when it was distilled from anything that would ferment, before rising to a respected place among the mixed drinks of the Victorian age – the fizzes, fixes and slings – and the strong, potent mixes of the cocktail age of the 1920s.

Gins of previous centuries would not be to the taste of present-day drinkers, for they were strongly flavoured and very sweet. During the 19th century London gained a reputation for its dry gin, which was distilled from the pure water from villages on the edge of the countryside such as Clerkenwell and Finsbury. London dry gin is now a generic term for unsweetened dry gin and, although it can be made anywhere in the world, some countries will only permit the description 'London dry' if the gin is imported from the United Kingdom. Plymouth gin, which can only be made in Plymouth, is a more aromatic, slightly sweetened gin. It has always been held in great affection by the Royal Navy, who have a tradition that true Pink Gin must be made with Plymouth gin. Dutch gin (which may be labelled Holland's or Geneva) has a fuller flavour still, while Sloe Gin (gin flavoured with sloes and sugar) is a bright clear red – delicious as an after-dinner drink.

The flavour of gin varies subtly from one brand to the next. It is also important when choosing a gin to look closely at the label. Some types are lower in alcohol than others (they range in percentage volume from 47.3 to 37.5%), resulting in a less potent drink. All alcoholic drinks contain congeners (the elements in alcohol that cause hangovers). There are fewer of these in colourless spirits such as vodka than in spirits like whisky and rum, and fewest of all in gin.

Gin makes an ideal base for cocktails because it blends well with other flavours, whets the appetite rather than dulling it and gives the drinker an instant lift. It is not for nothing that the most famous cocktail of all time – the Dry Martini – is a gin-based drink. Famous Dry Martini drinkers include Noel Coward, W C Fields, Dean Martin, Humphrey Bogart and Ernest Hemingway.

After the gin, ice is probably the most important ingredient in a cocktail. It has two functions, chilling the drink and acting as a beater in the shaker.

Crushed ice cools a drink more quickly than cracked ice, but dilutes it more rapidly. Always use tongs to transfer ice to glasses; using a spoon means that you risk adding water with the ice. When mixing drinks, clear drinks are normally stirred in a mixing glass, while cloudy drinks (those containing egg white, cream or fruit juices) are shaken in a blender or cocktail shaker and then strained, ideally into a chilled glass.

Sugar Syrup
This may be used instead of sugar to sweeten cocktails and to give them more body. It can be bought, but is simple to make at home.

Put 4 tablespoons of sugar and 4 tablespoons water in a small pan and stir over a low heat until the sugar has dissolved. Bring to the boil and boil, without stirring, for 1–2 minutes. Store in a sterilized bottle in the refrigerator for up to 2 months.

Classics

Dry Martini

New Orleans Dry Martini

Horse's Neck

Opera

Clover Club

Pink Clover Club

Albermarle Fizz

Bronx

White Lady

Maiden's Prayer

Monkey Gland

Paradise

French '75

Orange Blossom

Dry Martini

5–6 ice cubes
½ measure dry vermouth
3 measures gin
1 green olive

The Dry Martini, which was invented at the Knickerbocker Hotel in New York in 1910, has become the most famous cocktail of all. Lemon rind is sometimes used as a decoration instead of a green olive.

Put the ice cubes into a mixing glass. Pour the vermouth and gin over the ice and stir (never shake) vigorously and evenly without splashing, then strain into a chilled cocktail glass. Serve with a green olive.

Serves 1

New Orleans Dry Martini

5–6 ice cubes
2–3 drops pernod
1 measure dry vermouth
4 measures gin

Put the ice cubes into a mixing glass. Pour the pernod over the ice, then pour in the vermouth and gin. Stir (never shake) vigorously and evenly without splashing. Strain into a chilled cocktail glass.

Serves 1

Horse's Neck

4–6 ice cubes, cracked
1½ measures gin
dry ginger ale
long spiral of lemon rind

Put the ice into a tall glass and pour in the gin. Top up with dry ginger ale then dangle the lemon rind over the edge of the glass.

Serves 1

Variation

This classic cocktail can also be made with a brandy, rum or whisky base instead of gin. The spiral of lemon rind is essential.

Opera

4–5 ice cubes
1 measure Dubonnet
½ measure Curaçao
2 measures gin
orange rind spiral, to
    decorate

Put the ice cubes into a mixing
glass. Pour the Dubonnet,
Curaçao and gin over the ice. Stir
evenly, then strain into a chilled
cocktail glass. Decorate with the
orange rind spiral and serve.

Serves 1

Clover Club

4–5 ice cubes
juice of 1 lime
½ teaspoon sugar syrup
(see page 7)
1 egg white
3 measures gin

to decorate
grated lime rind
lime wedge

Put the ice cubes into a cocktail
shaker. Pour the lime juice, sugar
syrup, egg white and gin over the
ice and shake until a frost forms.
Strain into a tumbler and serve
decorated with grated lime rind
and a lime wedge.

Serves 1

Pink Clover Club

4–5 ice cubes
juice of 1 lime
dash of grenadine
1 egg white
3 measures gin
strawberry slice, to
decorate

Grenadine is a sweet non-alcoholic syrup made from pomegranates, which give it its rich rosy pink colour.

Put the ice cubes into a cocktail shaker. Pour the lime juice, grenadine, egg white and gin over the ice. Shake until a frost forms, then strain into a cocktail glass. Decorate with a strawberry slice and serve with a straw.

Serves 1

Albemarle Fizz

4–6 ice cubes
1 measure gin
juice of ½ lemon
2 dashes raspberry syrup
½ teaspoon sugar syrup
    (see page 7)
soda water
cocktail cherries, to
    decorate

Put 2-3 ice cubes into a mixing glass and add the gin, lemon juice, raspberry syrup and sugar syrup. Stir to mix then strain into a highball glass. Add 2-3 fresh ice cubes and top up with soda water. Decorate with two cherries on a cocktail stick and serve with straws.

Serves 1

Bronx

cracked ice
1 measure gin
1 measure sweet
    vermouth
1 measure dry vermouth
2 measures fresh orange
    juice

Place some cracked ice, the gin,
sweet and dry vermouths and
orange juice in a cocktail shaker.
Shake to mix. Pour into a small
glass, straining the drink if
preferred.

Serves 1

classics

White Lady

3–4 ice cubes
2 measures gin
1 measure Cointreau
1 teaspoon lemon juice
about ½ teaspoon egg
    white
spiral of lemon rind, to
    decorate

Place the ice cubes, gin, Cointreau, lemon juice and egg white in a cocktail shaker. Shake to mix then strain into a cocktail glass. Decorate with the spiral of lemon.

Serves 1

To make a Pink Lady, substitute 1 teaspoon grenadine for the Cointreau.

Maiden's Prayer

4–5 ice cubes
3 drops Angostura bitters
juice of 1 lemon
1 measure Cointreau
2 measures gin

Put the ice cubes into a cocktail shaker. Pour the bitters over the ice, add the lemon juice, Cointreau and gin and shake until a frost forms. Strain into a cocktail glass and serve with a straw.

Serves 1

Monkey Gland

1 measure orange juice
2 measures gin
3 dashes pernod
3 dashes grenadine
3–4 ice cubes

Put the orange juice, gin, pernod and grenadine into a cocktail shaker with 3-4 ice cubes. Shake well then strain into a chilled cocktail glass.

Serves 1

Paradise

2–3 ice cubes, cracked
1 measure gin
½ measure apricot brandy
½ measure fresh orange
    juice
dash of fresh lemon juice

to decorate
1 orange slice
1 lemon slice

Place the ice cubes in a cocktail
shaker and add the gin, apricot
brandy and orange and lemon
juices. Shake to mix then strain
into a cocktail glass. Decorate
with the orange and lemon slices.

Serves 1

French '75

cracked ice
1 measure gin
juice of ½ lemon
1 teaspoon caster sugar
chilled Champagne or
  sparkling dry white
  wine
orange slice, to decorate

'It hits the spot with remarkable precision', wrote a cocktail book eighty years ago about the French '75. It still does!

Half fill a tall glass with cracked ice. Add the gin, lemon juice and sugar and stir well. Top up with chilled Champagne and serve with an orange slice.

Serves 1

Orange Blossom

1 measure gin
1 measure sweet
    vermouth
1 measure fresh orange
    juice
2–3 ice cubes
orange slices, to
    decorate

**This is a cocktail from the
prohibition years, when it
was also sometimes
known as an Adirondack.
The orange juice could
disguise a hearty slug of
rotgut gin.**

Pour the gin, vermouth and
orange juice into a cocktail
shaker and shake to mix. Place
the ice cubes in a tumbler and
strain the cocktail over them.
Decorate the rim of the glass with
orange slices.

Serves 1

Exotic Cocktails

Crossbow

Gin Tropical

Long Island Iced Tea

Golden Dawn

Juliana Blue

Cherry Julep

Bijou

Night of Passion

Sapphire Martini

Peach Blow

Honolulu

Ben's Orange Cream

Crossbow

4–5 ice cubes
½ measure gin
½ measure crème de
    cacao
½ measure Cointreau
drinking chocolate
    powder, to decorate

Put the ice cubes into a cocktail shaker and add the gin, crème de cacao and Cointreau. Dampen the rim of a chilled cocktail glass with a little water then dip the rim into a saucer of drinking chocolate. Shake the drink vigorously then strain into the prepared glass.

Serves 1

Gin Tropical

4–6 ice cubes
1½ measures gin
1 measure fresh lemon
    juice
1 measure passion fruit
    juice
½ measure fresh orange
    juice
soda water
orange rind spiral, to
    decorate

Put 2–3 ice cubes into a cocktail shaker, pour in the gin, lemon juice, passion fruit juice and orange juice and shake well. Put 2–3 fresh ice cubes into an old-fashioned glass and strain the cocktail over the ice. Top up with soda water and stir gently. Decorate with an orange rind spiral.

Serves 1

Long Island Iced Tea

8 ice cubes
½ measure gin
½ measure vodka
½ measure white rum
½ measure tequila
½ measure Cointreau
1 measure lemon juice
½ teaspoon sugar syrup
    (see page 7)
cola, to top up
lemon slice, to decorate

Put 2 ice cubes into a mixing glass. Add the gin, vodka, rum, tequila, Cointreau, lemon juice and sugar syrup. Stir well, then strain into a tall glass almost filled with the remaining ice cubes. Top up with cola and decorate with the slice of lemon.

Serves 1

Golden Dawn

4–5 ice cubes
juice of ½ orange
1 measure Calvados
1 measure apricot brandy
3 measures gin
soda water
skewered orange rind, to
decorate

Put the ice cubes into a cocktail
shaker. Pour the orange juice,
Calvados, apricot brandy and gin
over the ice and shake until a
frost forms. Strain into a highball
glass, top up with soda water and
decorate with orange rind.

Serves 1

Juliana Blue

crushed ice
1 measure gin
½ measure Cointreau
½ measure blue Curaçao
2 measures pineapple
   juice
½ measure fresh lime
   juice
1 measure cream of
   coconut
1–2 ice cubes

to decorate
pineapple slice
cocktail cherries

Put some crushed ice into a blender and pour in the gin, Cointreau, blue Curaçao, pineapple and lime juices and cream of coconut. Blend at high speed for several seconds until the mixture has a consistency of soft snow. Put the ice cubes into a cocktail glass and strain the mixture on to them. Decorate with a pineapple slice and cocktail cherries. Serve with straws.

Serves 1

Cherry Julep

3–4 ice cubes
juice of ½ lemon
1 teaspoon sugar syrup
    (see page 7)
1 teaspoon grenadine
1 measure cherry brandy
1 measure sloe gin
2 measures gin
chopped ice
lemon rind strips, to
    decorate

Put the ice cubes into a cocktail shaker. Pour the lemon juice, sugar syrup, grenadine, cherry brandy, sloe gin and gin over the ice. Fill a highball glass with finely chopped ice. Shake the mixture until a frost forms then strain it into the ice-filled glass. Decorate with lemon rind strips and serve.

Serves 1

Bijou

3 ice cubes, cracked
1 measure gin
½ measure green
   Chartreuse
½ measure sweet
   vermouth
dash of orange bitters

to decorate
1 green olive
piece of lemon rind

Chartreuse is made by the Carthusian monks at their monastery near Grenoble, in the French Alps. The recipe is a secret but it is known to contain over 130 different herbs. There are two versions, green which is the stronger, and the weaker but sweeter yellow.

Put the ice cubes into a mixing glass and add the gin, Chartreuse, vermouth and bitters. Stir well and strain into a cocktail glass. Place the olive on a cocktail stick and add to the cocktail then squeeze the zest from the lemon rind over the surface.

Serves 1

Night of Passion

2 measures gin
1 measure Cointreau
1 tablespoon fresh lemon
    juice
2 measures peach nectar
2 tablespoons
    passionfruit juice
6–8 ice cubes

Put the gin, Cointreau, lemon juice, peach nectar and passionfruit juice into a cocktail shaker with 3–4 ice cubes and shake well. Strain into an old-fashioned glass over 3–4 fresh ice cubes.

Serves 1

Sapphire Martini

4 ice cubes
2 measures gin
½ measure blue Curaçao
1 red or blue cocktail
    cherry (optional)

Although blue Curaçao gives this drink its stunning colour, it is an orange flavoured liqueur.

Put the ice cubes into a cocktail shaker. Pour in the gin and blue Curaçao. Shake well to mix. Strain into a cocktail glass and carefully drop in a cocktail cherry, if using.

Serves 1

Peach Blow

8 cracked ice cubes
juice of ½ lemon or 1 lime
4 strawberries, crushed
1½ teaspoons caster
    sugar
1 tablespoon double
    cream
2 measures gin
soda water
strawberry slices, to
    decorate

**This recipe is deceptive.
Despite its name, it is
actually an alcoholic version
of strawberries and cream.**

Put 4 of the ice cubes into a
cocktail shaker, add the lemon
juice, strawberries, sugar, double
cream and gin and shake well.
Strain into a tall glass and top up
with soda water. Decorate with
strawberry slices.

Serves 1

Honolulu

4–5 ice cubes
1 measure pineapple
    juice
1 measure fresh lemon
    juice
1 measure fresh orange
    juice
½ teaspoon grenadine
3 measures gin

to decorate
pineapple slice
cocktail cherry

Put the ice cubes into a cocktail shaker. Pour the pineapple, lemon and orange juices, the grenadine and gin over the ice and shake until a frost forms. Strain the drink into a chilled cocktail glass and decorate with the pineapple and cherry.

Serves 1

Ben's Orange Cream

4–5 ice cubes
1 measure Cointreau
1 measure single cream
3 measures gin
1 tablespoon sugar syrup
    (see page 7)
chocolate flake, to
    decorate

Put the ice cubes into a cocktail shaker. Pour the Cointreau, cream and gin over the ice. Add the sugar syrup to the gin mixture and shake until a frost forms. Pour into a large glass and decorate with a chocolate flake.

Serves 1

Coolers & Fizzers

Gin Sling

4–5 ice cubes
juice of ½ lemon
1 measure cherry brandy
3 measures gin
soda water
cherries, to decorate
    (optional)

Put the ice cubes into a cocktail shaker. Pour the lemon juice, cherry brandy and gin over the ice and shake until a frost forms. Pour without straining into a hurricane glass and top up with soda water. Decorate with cherries, if liked, and serve with straws.

Serves 1

Gin Cup

coolers & fizzers

3 mint sprigs, extra to
  decorate
1 teaspoon sugar syrup
chopped ice
juice of ½ lemon
3 measures gin

Put the mint and sugar syrup into an old-fashioned glass and stir them about to bruise the mint slightly. Fill the glass with chopped ice, add the lemon juice and gin and stir until a frost begins to form. Decorate with extra mint sprigs.

Serves 1

Gin Cooler

3–4 ice cubes
½ teaspoon grenadine
juice of 1 lemon
3 measures gin
soda water

to decorate
1 cocktail cherry
1 lemon slice

Put the ice cubes into a highball glass. Pour the grenadine over the ice, then the lemon juice and the gin and stir evenly allowing the mixture to blend. Top up the drink with soda water. Decorate with a cocktail cherry and a lemon slice.

Serves 1

Gin Floradora

4–5 ice cubes
½ teaspoon sugar syrup
(see page 7)
juice of ½ lime
½ teaspoon grenadine
2 measures gin
dry ginger ale
twist of lime rind, to
decorate

Put the ice cubes into a cocktail shaker. Pour in the sugar syrup, lime juice, grenadine and gin and shake until a frost forms. Pour without straining into a hurricane glass. Top up with dry ginger ale, decorate with a lime twist and serve.

Serves 1

Sea Breeze

6–8 ice cubes
½ measure fresh
    grapefruit juice
½ measure cranberry
    juice
1 measure dry vermouth
3 measures gin
lime slice, to decorate

Put 2–3 ice cubes into a mixing glass. Pour the grapefruit juice, cranberry juice, vermouth and gin over the ice then stir gently. Put 4–5 fresh ice cubes into a chilled hurricane glass and strain the drink over the ice. Decorate with a lime slice.

Serves 1

Morning Glory Fizz

4–5 ice cubes

1 measure fresh lemon juice

½ teaspoon sugar syrup (see page 7)

3 measures gin

1 egg white

3 drops pernod

ginger ale

Put the ice cubes into a cocktail shaker. Pour the lemon juice, sugar syrup and gin over the ice. Add the egg white, then the pernod and shake until a frost forms. Strain into a chilled old-fashioned glass, top up with ginger ale and serve with a straw.

Serves 1

Variation

The Morning Glory Fizz can be made with whisky instead of gin.

60

Sydney Fizz

4–5 ice cubes
1 measure fresh lemon
   juice
1 measure fresh orange
   juice
½ teaspoon grenadine
3 measures gin
soda water
orange slice, to decorate

Put the ice cubes into a cocktail shaker. Pour the lemon and orange juices, grenadine and gin over the ice and shake vigorously until a frost forms. Strain into an old-fashioned glass. Top up with soda water, add the orange slice and serve.

Serves 1

Gin Fix

crushed ice cubes
1 tablespoon caster
    sugar
juice of ¼ lemon
1 measure water
2 measures gin
orange and lemon slices,
    to decorate

Fixes are also known as Daisies. They often contain large quantities of fruit or have lavish fruit decorations.

Fill a tall glass two-thirds full with crushed ice. Add the sugar, lemon juice, water and gin and stir well. Decorate the rim of the glass with orange and lemon slices.

Serves 1

coolers & fizzers

63

Singapore Gin Sling

6–8 ice cubes
juice of ½ lemon
juice of ½ orange
1 measure cherry brandy
3 measures gin
3 drops Angostura bitters
soda water
1 lemon slice, to
    decorate

Put 4–6 ice cubes into a cocktail shaker. Pour the lemon and orange juices, cherry brandy and gin over the ice and add the bitters. Shake the mixture until a frost forms. Put 2 fresh ice cubes into a hurricane glass. Pour the cocktail without straining into the glass and top up with soda water. Decorate with the lemon slice and serve.

Serves 1

Salty Dog

2–3 ice cubes
pinch of salt
1 measure gin
2–2½ measures fresh
   grapefruit juice
orange slice, to decorate

A Salty Dog can also be made with vodka. Sometimes the glass is rimmed with salt, like a Margarita.

Put the ice cubes into an old-fashioned glass. Put the salt on the ice and add the gin and grapefruit juice. Stir gently and serve. Decorate with an orange slice.

Serves 1

Honeydew

1 measure gin
½ measure fresh lemon
 juice
1 dash of pernod
50 g (2 oz) honeydew
 melon, diced
3–4 cracked ice cubes
Champagne

This is the drink to serve at the end of a late Sunday brunch – the combination of honeydew melon and gin makes the perfect transition from breakfast to lunchtime drinks.

Place the gin, lemon juice, pernod and melon in a blender and blend for 30 seconds, then pour into a large wine glass. Top up with Champagne.

Serves 1

John Collins

5–6 ice cubes
1 teaspoon sugar syrup
  (see page 7)
1 measure fresh lemon
  juice
3 measures gin
soda water

to decorate
1 lemon slice
1 mint sprig

The Collins is the tallest of the mixed drinks. It is made with a spirit, lemon juice and water. The John Collins, originally made with Holland's gin, was the first. Now there are also the Mick Collins (Irish whiskey), Pierre Collins (cognac) and the Pedro Collins (made with rum).

Put the ice cubes into a cocktail shaker. Pour in the sugar syrup, lemon juice and gin and shake vigorously until a frost forms. Pour without straining into a Collins glass. Add the lemon and mint and top up with soda water. Stir gently and serve.

Serves 1

Lime Gin Fizz

4–5 ice cubes
2 measures gin
1 measure lime cordial
soda water
lime wedges, to decorate

Put the ice cubes into a tall glass. Pour the gin and the lime cordial over the ice cubes. Top up with soda water, decorate with wedges of lime and serve with straws.

Serves 1

Pink Gin

1–4 dashes Angostura
    bitters
1 measure gin
iced water, to top up

Angostura bitters were developed in the South American town of Angostura in the 19th century. Originally intended for medicinal use, they were put into glasses of gin by the Royal Navy, thus inventing pink gin. Using orange bitters instead of Angostura transforms the drink into a Yellow Gin.

Shake the bitters into a cocktail glass and roll it around until the sides are well coated. Add the gin, then top up with iced water to taste.

Serves 1

High Spirits

Collinson

Alice Springs

Poet's Dream

Moon River

Knockout

Red Kiss

Kiss in the Dark

Earthquake

Burnsides

Woodstock

Stormy Weather

Luigi

Collinson

3 ice cubes, cracked
dash of orange bitters
1 measure gin
½ measure dry vermouth
¼ measure kirsch
piece of lemon rind

to decorate
½ strawberry
lemon slice

Put the ice cubes into a mixing glass, then add the bitters, gin, vermouth and kirsch. Stir well and strain into a cocktail glass. Squeeze the zest from the lemon rind over the surface, and decorate the rim of the glass with the strawberry and lemon.

Serves 1

Alice Springs

4–5 ice cubes
1 measure fresh lemon
   juice
1 measure fresh orange
   juice
½ teaspoon grenadine
3 measures gin
3 drops Angostura bitters
soda water
orange slice, to decorate

Put the ice cubes into a cocktail
shaker. Pour in the lemon juice,
orange juice, grenadine and gin.
Add the bitters and shake until a
frost forms. Pour into a tall glass
and top up with soda water.
Decorate with a slice of orange
and serve with straws.

Serves 1

Poet's Dream

4–5 ice cubes
1 measure Bénédictine
1 measure dry vermouth
3 measures gin
1 slice lemon rind

Bénédictine has been made for almost 500 years, originally by the monks of Fécamp Abbey. When mixed with an equal quantity of brandy it is known as a B&B.

Put the ice cubes into a mixing glass. Pour the Bénédictine, vermouth and gin over the ice and stir vigorously, without splashing. Strain into a chilled cocktail glass. Twist the lemon rind over the drink, drop it in and serve.

Serves 1

Moon River

4–5 ice cubes
½ measure dry gin
½ measure apricot brandy
½ measure Cointreau
¼ measure Galliano
¼ measure fresh lemon
    juice
cocktail cherry, to
    decorate

Put some ice cubes into a mixing glass and pour in the gin, apricot brandy, Cointreau, Galliano and lemon juice. Stir then strain the drink into a large chilled cocktail glass. Decorate with the cherry and serve.

Serves 4

Knockout

4–5 ice cubes
1 measure dry vermouth
½ measure white crème
    de menthe
2 measures gin
1 drop pernod
lemon slice, to serve

Crème de menthe is a sweetish mint-flavoured liqueur. It may be green or white, although the flavour remains the same. The white version is used here to blend with the milky colour of the pernod.

Put the ice cubes into a mixing glass. Pour the vermouth, crème de menthe and gin over the ice, stir vigorously, then strain into a chilled old-fashioned glass. Add the pernod and serve with a lemon slice.

Serves 1

Red Kiss

3 ice cubes, cracked
1 measure dry vermouth
½ measure gin
½ measure cherry brandy

to decorate
1 cocktail cherry
spiral of lemon rind

Put the ice cubes into a mixing glass, add the vermouth, gin and cherry brandy and stir well. Strain into a chilled cocktail glass and decorate with the cherry and spiral of lemon.

Serves 1

Kiss in the Dark

4–5 ice cubes
1 measure gin
1 measure cherry brandy
1 teaspoon dry vermouth

Put the ice cubes into a cocktail shaker and pour in the gin, cherry brandy and dry vermouth. Shake then strain into a chilled cocktail glass.

Serves 1

Earthquake

6–8 ice cubes
1 measure gin
1 measure whisky
1 measure pernod

This is an extremely potent concoction. Should an earthquake occur while you are drinking it, commented one 1920s cocktail book, it won't matter.

Put 3–4 ice cubes into a cocktail shaker. Add the gin, whisky and pernod and shake well. Strain into a cocktail glass and add 3–4 fresh ice cubes.

Serves 1

Burnsides

8–10 ice cubes
2 drops Angostura bitters
1 teaspoon cherry brandy
1 measure sweet
    vermouth
2 measures dry
    vermouth
2 measures gin
lemon rind strips, to
    decorate

Put 4–5 ice cubes into a cocktail shaker. Dash the bitters over the ice, add the cherry brandy, sweet and dry vermouths and gin. Shake lightly, then strain into a glass over the remaining ice cubes. Decorate with lemon rind strips.

Serves 1

Woodstock

2–3 ice cubes, crushed
1 measure gin
1 measure dry vermouth
¼ measure Cointreau
1 measure fresh orange
   juice

to decorate
piece of orange rind
orange slice

Put the ice into a cocktail shaker and add the gin, vermouth, Cointreau and orange juice. Shake to mix and strain into a cocktail glass. Squeeze the zest from the orange rind over the surface, and decorate with the orange slice.

Serves 1

Stormy Weather

3 ice cubes, cracked
1½ measures gin
¼ measure Mandarine
    Napoléon liqueur
¼ measure dry vermouth
¼ measure sweet
    vermouth
spiral of orange rind, to
    decorate

Mandarine Napoléon is a French tangerine-flavoured liqueur.

Put the ice cubes into a cocktail shaker and add the gin, Mandarine Napoléon and dry and sweet vermouths. Shake to mix and strain into a chilled cocktail glass. Decorate the rim of the glass with the spiral of orange.

Serves 1

Luigi

4–5 ice cubes
1 measure fresh orange
      juice
1 measure dry vermouth
½ measure Cointreau
1 measure grenadine
2 measures gin
orange slice, to decorate

Put the ice cubes into a mixing glass. Pour the orange juice, vermouth, Cointreau, grenadine and gin over the ice and stir vigorously. Strain into a chilled cocktail glass, decorate with the orange slice and serve.

Serves 1

INDEX

Acknowledgements

Octopus Publishing Group
  Ltd./Neil Mersh 2, 3, 11,
  16, 19, 23, 25, 30, 45, 49,
  53, 55, 59, 61, 67, 70, 72,
  74, 79, 83, 85, 93
  /Peter Myers 27, 37, 91
  /William Reavell Cover, 5,
  6-7, 8, 13, 15, 20, 28, 33,
  34, 39, 41, 47, 50, 57, 65,
  69, 77, 80, 87, 90
  /Simon Smith 42, 62